Grammar Practice

Grade 11

Table of Contents

Module 15   **SPELLING**

MODULE 1: PARTS OF SPEECH
NOUNS

The Eight Parts of Speech			
noun	adjective	pronoun	conjunction
verb	adverb	preposition	interjection

1a   **A *noun* is a word used to name a person, a place, a thing, or an idea.**

PERSONS	skater, Haruki Murakami, grandfather, police
PLACES	valley, Connecticut, nation, gymnasium
THINGS	apple, Grammy Award, fever, life, cactus
IDEAS	friendship, trust, worry, value, liberty

1b   **A *common noun* names any one of a group of persons, places, things, or ideas. A *proper noun* names a particular person, place, thing, or idea.**

COMMON NOUNS	woman, nation, event, holiday, language, car, bridge, road
PROPER NOUNS	Chien-Shiung Wu, China, Academy Awards, Valentine's Day, Italian, Toyota, London Bridge, Route 66

1c   **A *concrete noun* names an object that can be perceived by one or more of the senses (hearing, sight, smell, taste, or touch). An *abstract noun* names a quality, a characteristic, an emotion, or an idea.**

CONCRETE NOUNS	guitar, cafeteria, Idaho, Bob Ross, lamp
ABSTRACT NOUNS	skill, bravery, love, charm, solitude, humor

1d   **A *collective noun* names a group.**

COLLECTIVE NOUNS	class, swarm, fleet, crew, group, team

1e   **A *compound noun* consists of two or more words used together as a single noun. Some compound nouns are written as one word, some as separate words, and others as hyphenated words.**

COMPOUND NOUNS	sidewalk, telephone pole, bull's-eye, Jonas Salk

EXERCISE 1   Classifying Nouns

Classify each of the nouns below by writing *comm.* for *common* or *prop.* for *proper*. Then, if the noun is *compound*, write *comp.*, and if it is *collective*, write *coll.* Separate your answers with a semicolon.

EX. 1. family ____*comm.*; *coll.*____

1.	football	_____	11.	Japan	_____
2.	dancer	_____	12.	child	_____
3.	Pablo Picasso	_____	13.	team	_____
4.	hotel	_____	14.	Ohio	_____
5.	Buick	_____	15.	orange	_____
6.	Labor Day	_____	16.	sunflower	_____
7.	vegetable	_____	17.	shower	_____
8.	piano	_____	18.	totem pole	_____
9.	sister-in-law	_____	19.	South America	_____
10.	honesty	_____	20.	herd	_____

EXERCISE 2   Classifying Concrete and Abstract Nouns

On the line before each of the sentences below, classify each italicized noun. Write *con.* for *concrete* or *abs.* for *abstract*. Separate your answers with a semicolon.

EX. __*con.*; *abs.*__   1. The *coach* thanked the players for their *dedication* to the team.

_____   1. That *play* was written by *Tennessee Williams*.

_____   2. Abraham Lincoln earned a *reputation* for *honesty*.

_____   3. The *United Nations* tries to ensure world *peace*.

_____   4. Early on, Pablo Picasso showed great *talent* as an *artist*.

_____   5. Examples of *pasta* include *spaghetti*, macaroni, and penne.

_____   6. Horticulturists are *people* who study the art and science of growing fruits, vegetables, and *flowers*.

_____   7. Civil rights *laws* provide equal *opportunities* to all people.

_____   8. *Walter Cronkite* was a newscaster on *television*.

_____   9. Use *caution* when handling chemicals in the *laboratory*.

_____   10. In what *year* did the *wedding* of George and Martha Washington occur?

_____   11. The *audience* applauded the speaker's *ideas*.

_____   12. *Grapes* spilled out of the *bowl* and onto the table.

_____   13. The *sunset* was the color of a ripe *peach*.

_____   14. The *popularity* of the author was well known in *China*.

_____   15. His *success* was due to his *humor*.

PRONOUNS

1f   **A *pronoun* is a word used in place of a noun or of more than one noun.**

Personal Pronouns	I, me, my, mine, we, us, our, ours, you, your, yours, he, him, his, she, her, hers, it, its, they, them, their, theirs
Relative Pronouns	who, whom, whose, which, that
Interrogative Pronouns	who, whose, what, whom, which
Demonstrative Pronouns	this, that, these, those
Indefinite Pronouns	all, another, any, anybody, anyone, anything, both, each, either, everybody, everyone, everything, few, many, more, most, much, neither, no one, nobody, none, one, other, several, some, somebody, someone, such
Reflexive/ Intensive Pronouns	myself, oneself, ourselves, yourself, yourselves, himself, herself, itself, themselves

NOTE   In this book, the words *my, your, his, her, ours*, and *their* are considered possessive pronouns rather than adjectives. Follow your teacher's instructions in referring to such words.

A word that a pronoun stands for is called its ***antecedent.*** A pronoun may appear in the same sentence as its antecedent or in a following sentence. The antecedent may be a noun or another pronoun.

EXAMPLE   **They** went home. Kim followed **them.** [*They* is the antecedent of *them.*]

EXERCISE 3   Identifying Pronouns

Underline the pronouns in the following sentences.

EX. 1. Were <u>both</u> of Mia's parents born in Taiwan?

1. Those are the boots Jim bought yesterday.
2. Would you like more salad?
3. A few of Sally's friends have planned a surprise party.
4. W. H. Auden was the poet who wrote "The Composer."
5. Rafael built that computer table himself.
6. Everyone on the debating team is ready to begin.
7. Now extinct, the *Dunkleosteus* was a fish that was as big as a bus.

8. This is the phone number to call if the girls want to order some sandwiches.
9. Are the books on the dining room table mine?
10. The following morning, neither of the cars would start.
11. Anything we asked of Mr. and Mrs. Tong, they gave us gladly.
12. Since it was so late, the boys decided to sleep over, not trusting themselves to stay awake during the long drive home.
13. My parents say that much of the time young people watch television.
14. If you want it done right, I advise you to do it yourself.
15. Which of the computers has the software for teaching graphing?

EXERCISE 4   Identifying Pronouns and Their Antecedents

Underline the pronouns in the paragraph below. Underline the antecedent of each pronoun twice.

EX.   [1] <u>Grandma Moses</u> began painting when <u>she</u> was seventy-six years old.

[1] Grandma Moses' colorful pictures are valued today because they are filled with innocence and have a fresh, primitive style. [2] Many of the paintings hang in art museums. [3] Each of the scenes has a rural setting. [4] Grandma Moses based the paintings on memories she had of her childhood. [5] They were fond memories of a peaceful life on farms in Virginia and northern New York. [6] Several of the paintings show busy people, working and having fun. [7] Some are working in the fields or picking apples or hanging quilts out on a clothesline. [8] Grandma Moses taught herself to paint. [9] She never took art lessons; she apparently never needed them. [10] Grandma Moses lived 101 years, and in her last year, she painted twenty-five pictures.

ADJECTIVES

1g   An *adjective* is a word used to modify a noun or pronoun.

To *modify* means "to describe or to make more definite" the meaning of a word. Adjectives modify nouns or pronouns by telling *what kind, which one*, or *how many/how much*.

What kind?	**old** book, **blue** sky, **warm** water
Which one?	**that** game, **those** lights, **his** radio
How many?	**six** days, **nine** judges, **many** friends

The most frequently used adjectives are *a, an*, and *the*. These words are called **articles.**

A and *an* are **indefinite articles.** They indicate that a noun refers to one of a general group. *A* is used before words beginning with a consonant sound; *an* is used before words beginning with a vowel sound. *An* is also used before words beginning with the consonant *h* when the *h* is not pronounced.

EXAMPLES   **A** lion crouched in the tall grass.
             This is **an** excellent essay, Clarice!
             An hour passed while we chose **a** hat for the scarecrow.

The is the **definite article.** It indicates that a noun refers to someone or something in particular.

EXAMPLE   **The** blackbird sat in **the** cedar tree, sheltered from **the** rain.

Sometimes nouns are used as adjectives.

EXAMPLES   Have you ever been to an **auto** race? [*Auto*, usually a noun, is used as an adjective modifying the noun *race*.]
             Is that machine the new **carpet** cleaner? [*Carpet*, usually a noun, is used as an adjective modifying the noun *cleaner*.]

NOTE   Some pairs or groups of nouns are considered compound nouns. By checking a dictionary, you can avoid confusing a noun that is used as an adjective with a noun that is part of a compound noun.

       EXAMPLES   country club, blood bank, road map, United States

EXERCISE 5   Identifying Adjectives in Sentences

Underline the adjectives in each of the sentences below, and double underline the word each adjective modifies. Do not include *a, an*, or *the*.

   EX.   1. Onesimus developed a <u>successful</u> <u><u>cure</u></u> for smallpox in 1721.

   1. Smallpox is a serious disease that causes a high fever.
   2. Also a contagious disease, it was causing many people to die at the time.
   3. Onesimus based the new medicine on an old remedy he knew.
   4. That remedy had been a popular and common medicine in Africa.
   5. Onesimus was an enslaved African American.
   6. The Puritan leader who owned Onesimus sent the medicine to a Dr. Boylston.
   7. Dr. Boylston tried the remarkable medicine on three smallpox victims.
   8. The sick people became well.
   9. Onesimus did not receive immediate credit for his tremendous discovery.
   10. The dishonest Dr. Boylston took all credit for himself.

EXERCISE 6   Using Adjectives in Sentences

In each sentence below, add interesting adjectives to modify the nouns and pronouns. Write your sentences on your own paper.

   EX.   1. The workers took the truck to the building.
         1. *The fatigued workers took the rusty, old-fashioned truck to the gigantic building.*

   1. Scott gave a book to his father.
   2. Camara donated toys and tools for the sale.
   3. Marian packed a lunch for the picnic.
   4. The athlete ran across the field.
   5. The warrior fought the animal and rescued the child.
   6. Which book have you chosen for your report?
   7. For days, the woman made her baskets.
   8. During the day, we washed cars and raked the leaves.
   9. The children gave gifts to their friends at the party.
   10. Rosie painted a picture of the meadow for her relatives.

VERBS

1h   A *verb* is a word that expresses action or a state of being.

(1)   An *action verb* expresses physical or mental activity.

EXAMPLES   leap, sail, break, scoop, consider, forget, hope, believe

(2)   A *transitive verb* is an action verb that takes an *object*—a word that tells who or what receives the action.

EXAMPLES   The cows **crossed** the pasture. [The action of the verb *crossed* is received by *pasture*.]
Tyrone **tuned** his car's engine. [The action of the verb *tuned* is received by *engine*.]

(3)   An *intransitive verb* is an action verb that does not take an object.

EXAMPLES   The children **laughed.**
A letter **came** from your friend in Norway.

A verb can be transitive in one sentence and intransitive in another.

EXAMPLES   Shulka **wrote** a play. [transitive]
Shulka **wrote** carefully. [intransitive]

(4)   A *linking verb*, or *state-of-being verb*, connects the subject with a word that identifies or describes it.

The most commonly used linking verbs are forms of the verb *be: am, is, are, was, were, being*, and *been*. Other common linking verbs include *appear, become, feel, grow, look, remain, seem, smell, sound, stay, taste*, and *turn*.

EXAMPLES   This tree **is** a sycamore.
That music **sounds** distorted.

Many linking verbs can be used as action verbs as well.

EXAMPLES   The chicken **tasted** good. [The verb links the subject, *chicken*, to a word that describes it, *good*.]
Did you **taste** the chicken? [The verb describes an action taken by the subject, *you*.]

(5)   A *verb phrase* consists of a *main verb* and at least one *helping*, or *auxiliary*, *verb*. Common helping verbs are forms of *be*, forms of *have*, forms of *do*, and the auxiliaries *can, could, may, might, must, shall, should, will*, and *would*.

EXAMPLES   **did** speak, **must have been** sleeping, **is** working

EXERCISE 7   Identifying and Classifying Transitive and Intransitive Verbs

In the sentences below, underline each verb or verb phrase. Then identify the verb as transitive or intransitive. Write *trans.* for *transitive* or *intr.* for *intransitive* on the line before each sentence.

    EX. 1.   *intr.*   Marc <u>grew</u> tall.

_____ 1. The veterinarian treated my cat.

_____ 2. Georgia streamed a movie last night.

_____ 3. You skate particularly well.

_____ 4. Nadine is calling the dentist for an appointment.

_____ 5. I have grown many herbs in pots on my windowsill.

_____ 6. The twins are racing down the hill.

_____ 7. When did the bus leave?

_____ 8. For a three-year-old, Harley speaks very clearly.

_____ 9. Uncle Pierre drove to Texas last summer in an old car.

_____ 10. I named my cat "Humphrey" in honor of Humphrey Bogart.

EXERCISE 8   Identifying Verb Phrases and Helping Verbs

In each sentence below, underline the verb phrase once and the helping verb or verbs twice.

    EX. 1. Everyone in the auditorium <u>was cheering</u> for Tia.

1. Tomorrow we are starting a new literature selection.
2. I have been studying German for two years now.
3. Did Marilyn give you her new phone number?
4. He must have been hoping for a raise in pay.
5. The trees in the meadow have dropped their leaves.
6. We might go to the park after the game.
7. Does Andrew watch *Jeopardy* every night?
8. Benji would like more broccoli.
9. You should have seen the hot-air balloon in the field last night.
10. I must have lost my library card.

ADVERBS

1i An *adverb* is a word used to modify a verb, an adjective, or another adverb.

Adverbs modify by telling *how, when, where*, or *to what extent*.

How?	The rescue team worked **frantically.** The drummer plays **well.**
When?	Will winter be here **soon?** I **occasionally** play basketball.
Where?	The shutters flew **open.** Do ospreys travel **far?**
To what extent?	Cleve **nearly** won the race! I've **never** seen an ocean.

EXAMPLES The bank closes **promptly** each day. [*Promptly* modifies the verb *closes*, telling *when* the bank closes.]
I thought that the play was **rather** exciting. [*Rather* modifies the adjective *exciting*, telling *to what extent*.]
The police officer acted **quite** heroically. [*Quite* modifies the adverb *heroically*, telling *to what extent*.]

EXERCISE 9   Identifying Adverbs and the Words They Modify

Underline the adverbs in each of the following sentences. Draw brackets around the words they modify. Then identify the words modified by writing *v.* for *verb, adj.* for *adjective*, or *adv.* for *adverb* on the line before the sentence.

EX. ___*adj.*___ 1. Joseph Bruchac is a <u>nationally</u> [famous] storyteller.

_____ 1. The trash barrel is nearly empty.

_____ 2. My cousins from Nevada visit frequently.

_____ 3. Suddenly, all the bright lights dimmed.

_____ 4. We never found the lost necklace.

_____ 5. They finished their meeting quite quickly.

_____ 6. Geraldo and Demi were thoroughly happy with the results.

_____ 7. Did you play well in yesterday's game?

_____ 8. Turn the lever slowly so you don't break it.

_____ 9. Fish are rarely caught in this river.

_____ 10. These lines are slightly uneven.

_____ 11. Quite soon, we will have the election results.

_____ 12. The sheep grazed in a gently rolling meadow.

_____ 13. You can put the stack of boxes here.

_____ 14. Did you ever meet a famous person?

_____ 15. The food at that Chinese restaurant is really great.

EXERCISE 10   Using Adverbs in Sentences

Complete each sentence below by writing an appropriate adverb on the line provided. The word or phrase in parentheses tells you what information the adverb should give about the verb, adjective, or other adverb.

EX. 1. I have _almost_ finished my book. (*To what extent?*)

1. They will return the books _____. (*When?*)

2. Barbara picked up the papers _____. (*How?*)

3. John Wayne _____ played tough characters. (*When?*)

4. Sit _____. (*Where?*)

5. My friends _____ recognized me in my costume. (*To what extent?*)

6. This story was _____ exciting. (*To what extent?*)

7. The players on the opposing team played _____. (*How?*)

8. The package should arrive _____. (*When?*)

9. I'll put your sandwich _____. (*Where?*)

10. Kacey visits her older sister at college _____. (*When?*)

11. Helen speaks _____ quickly. (*To what extent?*)

12. The flock of geese are nesting _____. (*Where?*)

13. He has _____ visited Puerto Rico. (*When?*)

14. _____ gently, Jonah bandaged my arm. (*To what extent?*)

15. _____, I agreed to be president of the club. (*How?*)

MODULE 1: PARTS OF SPEECH
REVIEW EXERCISE 1

A.   Identifying Nouns, Pronouns, and Adjectives

On your own paper, identify the italicized words in each of the sentences below by writing *n.* for *noun, pron.* for *pronoun,* or *adj.* for *adjective.*

> EX. 1. *Those* are the *best* amplifiers on the market today.
>   1. *pron.; adj.*

1. *We* went for a *long* hike around Lake Sunapee.
2. Fern still remembers the *friends* she made in *Iran.*
3. The *woods* were peaceful and *dark.*
4. Please fill out the application with your *full* name and *address.*
5. The *Liberty Bell* is near Independence Hall in *Philadelphia.*
6. *Everyone* on the bus was anxious to get to the *next* station on time.
7. I wish that *I* had continued my *piano* lessons.
8. Eleanor had bought the *latest* newspapers for her *mother* to read.
9. He couldn't find *either* of his *shoes.*
10. Is *it* a fact that elephants have *remarkable* memories?

B.   Classifying Verbs

On the line before each of the following sentences, identify the italicized verb as an action verb or a linking verb. If it is an action verb, tell whether it is transitive or intransitive. Write *a.v.* for *action verb, l.v.* for *linking verb, trans.* for *transitive,* and *intr.* for *intransitive.*

> EX. <u>*a.v., intr.*</u> 1. They *were calling* to the hikers on the rocky slopes.

_____   1. People *are* often happy when they find unexpected treats.

_____   2. The bread *seems* slightly stale, don't you think?

_____   3. Where *did* you *buy* that silly hat?

_____   4. The students *remained* in their seats after the performance.

_____   5. The cat *sat* outside most of the day, enjoying the sunshine.

_____   6. Who *has borrowed* my tennis racquet?

_____   7. They *became* worried when the hikers did not return.

_____   8. *Do* you *remember* all of your lines for the play?

_____   9. Katya *worked* hard all afternoon, raking leaves.

_____ 10. It seems late; what time *is* it?

C. Identifying Adjectives and Adverbs

On the line before each sentence below, identify the italicized words by writing *adj.* for *adjective* or *adv.* for *adverb*. Then underline the word or words that each adjective modifies, and double underline the word or words each adverb modifies.

EX. *adv.; adj.* 1. Rather *quickly, black* <u>clouds</u> <u>appeared</u> in the sky.

_____ 1. *Humorous* advertisements *often* appear on television.

_____ 2. The game *certainly* ended in a *surprising* way.

_____ 3. Thank you for your *extremely thoughtful* letter.

_____ 4. *Yesterday* we saw a *young* bear close to our tent!

_____ 5. *Usually* you have to work hard to become a *great* athlete.

_____ 6. Tyrone finished the *history* project *easily*.

_____ 7. I had *hardly* begun to speak when an *older* gentleman interrupted me.

_____ 8. We were *very* happy to hear about the *Latin* award that you won!

_____ 9. *Unexpectedly*, a visitor arrived at the *information* booth just before closing time.

_____ 10. Ramón *unexpectedly* brought up *several* interesting questions at the meeting.

_____ 11. *Certainly*, water helps young plants to develop *strong* roots.

_____ 12. I did *not* know that Sandra Day O' Connor was the *first* woman to serve on the U.S. Supreme Court.

_____ 13. The *mushroom* soup was *truly* delicious.

_____ 14. Does popcorn *really* contain any *nutritional* value?

_____ 15. The *church* bus usually arrives at this corner *promptly* at 6:00 A.M.

_____ 16. How *often* do you watch the *evening* news on television?

_____ 17. The senators were *quite firm* in their support of the president.

_____ 18. Walking can *certainly* be an *excellent* form of exercise.

_____ 19. *Clearly*, I understand your *unusual* point of view.

_____ 20. *Yesterday* we visited the Smithsonian Institution in Washington, D. C., and stayed at a *nearby* hotel.

PREPOSITIONS

1j **A *preposition* is a word that shows the relationship of a noun or pronoun to some other word in the sentence.**

A preposition always introduces a *phrase*. The noun or pronoun that ends a prepositional phrase is the ***object of the preposition.*** In each of the following examples, the object of the preposition is *me*. Notice how the prepositions show six different relationships between *sang* and *me*.

EXAMPLES   Sabrina sang **to** me.   Sabrina sang **after** me.
                   Sabrina sang **with** me. Sabrina sang **before** me.
                   Sabrina sang **for** me.   Sabrina sang **beside** me.

Commonly Used Prepositions				
aboard	before	by	like	through
about	behind	concerning	near	to
above	below	down	of	toward
across	beneath	during	off	under
after	beside	except	on	until
against	besides	for	onto	up
along	between	from	outside	upon
among	beyond	in	over	with
around	but (meaning *except*)	inside	past	within
at		into	since	without

NOTE   The same word may be either an adverb or a preposition, depending on its use in a sentence.

EXAMPLES   A motorcycle zoomed **by.** [adverb]
                   A motorcycle zoomed **by** us. [preposition]

Prepositions can also be compound.

Compound Prepositions		
according to	in addition to	next to
because of	in front of	on account of
aside from	instead of	prior to

EXERCISE 11   Identifying Prepositions and Their Objects

Underline each preposition in the sentences below. Draw a bracket around its object.

EX. 1. Tony Thornton competed <u>for</u> an important boxing [title].

1. Tony Thornton was an African American mail carrier who worked in New Jersey.
2. He delivered mail to over four hundred homes.
3. In addition to that job, Tony had another large interest and talent.
4. He was a contender for the super-middleweight boxing championship.
5. Tony is a lifetime resident of New Jersey.
6. In one boxing match in 1993, Tony faced James Toney, a much younger boxer.
7. Tony boxed well, but he lost the match in a twelve-round decision.
8. Tony's co-workers at the post office sometimes made some good-natured jokes.
9. Because of his two interests, they called him "The Punching Postman."
10. However, his co-workers also shared great respect for Tony.
11. They agreed that he was a dedicated postal worker who never let his job suffer because of his boxing talent.
12. Before a boxing match, Tony spent many hours training.
13. He sometimes missed work after a match, though.
14. Usually, instead of resting, Tony delivered the mail the very next morning!
15. His co-workers supported Tony, whether he became the super-middleweight champion of the world or not.

EXERCISE 12   Describing an Amusement Park

You have been employed by a large entertainment company to plan a new amusement park. On your own paper, draw a diagram of the park. Show what rides, forms of entertainment, restaurants, and other attractions might be found there. Then, also on your own paper, write fifteen sentences describing the park. Use at least ten prepositions in your sentences, and include at least three compound prepositions. Underline the prepositions you use.

EX. 1. *<u>Inside</u> the park <u>next to</u> a Stone Age man, stands a giant statue <u>of</u> a prehistoric mammoth.*

MODULE 1: PARTS OF SPEECH
CONJUNCTIONS AND INTERJECTIONS

1k   A *conjunction* is a word used to join words or groups of words.

(1) *Coordinating conjunctions* join words or groups of words used in the same way.

Coordinating Conjunctions
and   but   for   nor   or   so   yet

EXAMPLES   The workshop has a bench saw **and** a sander in one corner.
             Advance ticket sales were slow, **but** many people showed up at the door.

(2) *Correlative conjunctions* are used in pairs to join words or groups of words used in the same way.

Correlative Conjunctions		
both … and	neither … nor	whether … or
either … or	not only … but (also)	

EXAMPLES   **Both** moose **and** caribou live in the north country.
             The comedian's routine was **not only** funny **but also** appropriate to the
             occasion.

(3) A *subordinating conjunction* begins a subordinate clause and connects it to an independent clause.

Commonly Used Subordinating Conjunctions			
after	because	since	when
although	before	so that	whenever
as	even though	than	where
as if	how	that	wherever
as much as	if	though	whether
as though	in order that	unless	while
as well as	provided	until	why

EXAMPLES   Did Otto decide **whether** he would take that class?
             We should take a taxi **since** the bus is late.

11   An *interjection* is a word that expresses emotion. It has no grammatical relation to other words in the sentence.

An interjection is set off from the rest of the sentence by an exclamation point or a comma.

EXAMPLES   **Hey!** Watch out for that truck!
No, there aren't many stars out tonight.

EXERCISE 13   Identifying and Classifying Conjunctions

Underline the conjunctions in the sentences below. In the space above each conjunction, write *coor.* for *coordinating conjunction*, *corr.* for *correlative conjunction*, or *sub.* for *subordinating conjunction*.

                                                                        coor.
EX. 1. Lee Seong Chul was a great spiritual leader, <u>and</u> he inspired many people.

1. Until Uncle Jeff bought the farm, he lived in the city.

2. Some students will finish the story before the class is over.

3. When Stephanie was born, the whole family sent flowers.

4. Horses, donkeys, and ponies ran freely in the pasture.

5. Mexico is a country of both ancient, abandoned cities and new, busy centers.

6. The people of River Junction, where I grew up, always looked out for all the young people.

7. Dad sang the song and made up the words.

8. Not only giant pandas but also red pandas live in bamboo forests in the mountains of Asia.

9. Gina said her essay was too long, yet we all agreed that it was wonderful.

10. Legend has it that the emperor Nero played the fiddle while the city of Rome burned.

EXERCISE 14   Using Interjections

On your own paper, write a sentence using each of the interjections below.

EX. 1. hey

    1. *Hey! Haven't I seen you on television?*

1. ouch	3. well	5. oh	7. why	9. ah
2. help	4. yes	6. wow	8. whew	10. ugh

1m	The part of speech of a word is determined by the way the word is used in a sentence.
EXAMPLES	Menino will win the election. You can **bank** on it. [*Bank* is used as a verb.]
	Deposit your paycheck in the **bank.** [*Bank* is used as a noun.]

EXERCISE 15   Classifying the Parts of Speech

Above each italicized word in the paragraph below, write the word's part of speech. Write *n.* for *noun, pron.* for *pronoun, v.* for *verb, adj.* for *adjective, adv.* for *adverb, prep.* for *preposition, conj.* for *conjunction*, or *intj.* for *interjection*.

               adj

EX.   [1] Gina heard a *loud* crash.

[1] Gina *ran* to the *open* window. [2] *Outside*, the wind was howling *and* shaking the shutters of her old house. [3] At first, she couldn't see *what* had caused the *crash* that she had heard. [4] "I'd better go *outside* and have a *look.*" [5] A large, *knotted* oak tree, planted by *her* grandfather many years ago, had fallen to the ground. [6] *"No!* It's just horrible, you beautiful old tree," *she* said. [7] *After* the storm, Gina helped her grandfather saw the *branches* and trunk of the tree into firewood. [8] As he worked, he said, *"That* was a great tree, almost like a dear friend, and I'll *surely* miss it." [9] For the *rest* of the fall and the cold winter months that followed, the yard *seemed* empty and sad without the oak tree. [10] Although *neither* of them spoke about it, the loss of their "old friend" *saddened* Gina and her grandfather. [11] Then, one *spring* morning, Gina saw a brand-new oak tree, which had sprouted from a *buried* acorn. [12] Gina rushed *into* the house and gave a *shout* to her grandfather. [13] *When* her grandfather saw the tiny seedling, he said, "Let's water it *well* and *put* a little fence around it to

keep it safe." [14] *Both* of them knew that *oak* trees take years and years to grow into

big trees. [15] But that didn't matter, *for* the seedling seemed *like* a gift from the

old tree.

MODULE 1: PARTS OF SPEECH
REVIEW EXERCISE 2

A.   Identifying Parts of Speech

In the paragraph below, identify the part of speech of each italicized word. Write *n.* for *noun, pron.* for *pronoun, v.* for *verb, adj.* for *adjective, adv.* for *adverb, prep.* for *preposition, conj.* for *conjunction,* or *intj.* for *interjection.*

v.   *prep.*

EX.   [1] If pets *crowd* your home, take a lesson *from* Sandee Chreiman.

[1] *This* Pennsylvania woman cares for forty-three animals in her *home*. [2] She doesn't find *all* those animals a *bother*. In fact, she thinks of them as a big, happy family. [3] *Yes*, some of them *sometimes* get into mischief. [4] *Some*, like the twelve cats and the five *dogs*, may occasionally jump on the furniture. [5] Others, such as the twenty-four ferrets, steal little items found *around* the house and hide *them* under Sandee's dresser. [6] Her *pet* bird watches all this activity from a *perch* overhead, while her pet rat sits quietly, munching on raisins. [7] *All* of Sandee's pets are special to her, but perhaps the ferrets are the *most* special. [8] Sandee has rescued many *pet* ferrets from *animal* shelters. [9] *Too* many people buy ferrets as pets and then decide *that* they don't want the animals. [10] Although ferrets are timid animals, *when* they are frightened, they may bite. [11] *That* is usually when the pet owner *takes* the ferret to a shelter. [12] Sandee rarely gets bitten by her *friendly* ferrets, *for* she understands that they need gentle care. [13] At Sandee's house, *that* care involves big, airy cages in an *upstairs* bedroom. [14] Because the ferrets *enjoy* running and playing, Sandee often opens the cages and lets the ferrets run *through* the house. [15] The ferrets have many friends among the five dogs, who often *let* the ferrets ride *around* the house on their backs.

B. Describing Your Personal Flag

A nation's flag often has special symbols on it that tell about the nation and about the beliefs of its people. Design a flag for yourself that has four sections. The flag should tell about you. On your own paper, write a short paragraph of at least ten sentences describing your personal flag. Use and label each of the eight parts of speech at least once.

> EX. *The top two sections of my personal <u>flag</u> represent my personality <u>and</u> my dreams. One part has a red rose in it; the other has a beautiful bird.*
>
>   *n.*   *conj.*

A.   Identifying Nouns, Pronouns, and Adjectives in Sentences

Classify each italicized word in the sentences below by writing *n.* for *noun, pron.* for *pronoun*, or *adj.* for *adjective* above the word. For each adjective, circle the word it modifies.

              n.   adj.   adj.   n.
EX. 1. Garrett Augustus Morgan invented many valuable tools.

1. *His* mother, Elizabeth Reed Morgan, was a *former* slave with African and Native

   American ancestry.

2. He sold his first invention, a tool to tighten *belts* on sewing machines, for *fifty*

   dollars.

3. Morgan invented a *fireproof* hood; attached to it was a small tank carrying *fresh*

   air.

4. *This* hood eventually became the gas mask, *which* Morgan patented in 1914.

5. Another invention that made Morgan famous was the automatic *traffic* light.

B.   Determining the Parts of Speech of Words

In the following paragraph, identify the part of speech of each italicized word or expression. On the line before each sentence, write *n.* for *noun, adj.* for *adjective, pron.* for *pronoun, v.* for *verb, adv.* for *adverb, prep.* for *preposition, conj.* for *conjunction*, or *intj.* for *interjection*.

EX.   [1]   *prep.*   Wherever I go, I buy a postcard *for* my album.

[1] _____ *Last* year, I went to Chicago to visit my cousin Sheila.

[2] _____ I bought a card that had a picture of the Art Institute on *it*.

[3] _____ *Outside* the museum's main entrance are two gigantic statues.

[4] _____ *Each* one is a lion. [5] _____ They *guard* the museum like

silent, powerful friends. [6] _____ *According to* the card, the lions were created by an American sculptor named Edward Kemeys. [7] _____ *Since* that trip, I have collected other postcards with statues and monuments on them. [8] _____ My *favorite* grandfather sent me a postcard from Paris. [9] _____ *Because* he knew of my interest in monuments, his card pictured the Arc de Triomphe. [10] _____ I've *never* before seen a monument in such a busy place. [11] _____ *Wow*! The card says that twelve major avenues meet in the circle surrounding the arch. [12] _____ My grandfather's note said that all those roads can create a *traffic* nightmare. [13] _____ The monument celebrates the *courage* of the soldiers of Napoleon, a historic leader of France. [14] _____ Along the monument's *outside* walls are a group of statues by the French sculptor François Rude. [15] _____ A flame that will burn *forever* has been installed beneath the arch to honor France's Unknown Soldier.

C.   Writing Sentences with Words Used as Specific Parts of Speech

On your own paper, write fifteen sentences according to the guidelines below. Underline the part of speech that has been asked for in each sentence.

> EX. 1. Use *down* as a preposition.
>   1. *The river flows <u>down</u> the hill.*

1. Use *some* as an adjective.
2. Use *so* as an adverb.
3. Use *touch* as a noun.
4. Use *where* as an interrogative pronoun.
5. Use *where* as a subordinating conjunction.
6. Use *by* as a preposition.
7. Use *outside* as an adverb.
8. Use *because of* as a compound preposition.
9. Use *either ... or* as a correlative conjunction.
10. Use *oh* as an interjection.
11. Use *taste* as a linking verb.
12. Use *might* as a helping verb.
13. Use *cover* as a verb.
14. Use *cover* as a noun.
15. Use *but* as a coordinating conjunction.

SUBJECTS AND PREDICATES

2a A sentence consists of two parts: a *subject* and a *predicate*. A *subject* tells *whom* or *what* the sentence is about. A *predicate* tells something about the subject.

| | PRED. | s. | PRED. |

EXAMPLES   When do | autumn leaves | fall from the branches of the trees?

In this example, the words labeled *subject* make up the **complete subject**. The words labeled *predicate* make up the **complete predicate**. Notice that parts of the complete predicate can come before and after the subject.

2b A *simple subject* is the main word or group of words in the complete subject that tells *whom* or *what* the sentence is about.

                        s.

EXAMPLES   Who was the research <u>scientist</u> on this project?

                        s.

                Decorating the float, the <u>students</u> kept warm with mittens and mugs of hot tea.

NOTE   In this book, the term *subject* refers to the simple subject unless otherwise indicated.

2c A *simple predicate* is a verb or verb phrase in the complete predicate that tells something about the subject.

                PRED.

EXAMPLES   Alfredo <u>wrote</u> clearly and eloquently.

                PRED.   PRED.

                <u>Did</u> Julia ever <u>find</u> the concert tickets?

NOTE   In this book, the term *verb* refers to the simple predicate (a one-word verb or a verb phrase) unless otherwise indicated.

EXERCISE 1   Identifying Complete Subjects and Simple Subjects in Sentences

In each of the following sentences, underline the complete subject once and the simple subject twice.

    EX. 1. <u>The old <u>sleigh</u></u> provided the only transportation during the blizzard.

1. The energetic kitten unraveled the ball of yarn.

2. My lab partner completed the science project on time.

3. Each member brought a list of suggestions to the meeting.

4. The orange chrysanthemums brightened Mr. Hwang's autumn garden.

5. Fresh dandelion greens are tasty in a salad.

6. Mrs. Wharton hoped for a better view of the purple martin.

7. At the track meet, Derek, along with Kate and Gloria, broke several records.

8. After ripping up the carpet, Donna refinished the wooden floors.

9. Piles of red and gold leaves covered the lawn, the driveway, and the front porch steps.

10. Dusty bookcases lined the walls of the abandoned house.

EXERCISE 2   Identifying Complete Predicates and Verbs in Sentences

In each sentence below, underline the complete predicate once and the verb twice. Be sure to include all parts of a verb phrase.

EX. 1. Today we will clean the entire apartment.

1. Yesterday we were walking by the new museum.

2. Angela bought large bags of birdseed at the supermarket.

3. On Saturday George took fresh bread to his neighbors.

4. We will make a quilt from those colorful scraps of fabric.

5. I am learning about everyday life in Israel.

6. Julian saw frogs and fish in the pond behind Robin's house.

7. Nell wanted answers immediately.

8. I have requested dozens of my favorite songs.

9. I gave Josephine fresh corn, tomatoes, and lettuce.

10. Jerry and I will baby-sit this weekend.

11. Into the compost pile Kim dumped the vegetable scraps.

12. Did Randy go outdoors to help his father?

13. Katy volunteered at the library.

14. All the seedlings grew into huge vines with plump pumpkins.

15. Each of the visitors remarked on the interesting new exhibit at the Museum of Modern Art.

COMPOUND SUBJECTS AND COMPOUND VERBS

2d   A *compound subject* consists of two or more subjects that are joined by a conjunction and have the same verb.

                                COMP. S.   V.
EXAMPLES   <u>The luggage</u> and <u>its contents</u> | <u>were damaged</u> in the storm.
                                COMP. S.   V.
            <u>Jamal, Terry,</u> and <u>Wanda</u> | <u>raced</u> to the finish line.

2e   A *compound verb* consists of two or more verbs or verb phrases that are joined by a conjunction and have the same subject.

                                    S.   COMP. V.
EXAMPLES   For enjoyment <u>Vince</u> | <u>reads</u> or <u>plays</u> basketball.
                            S.   COMP. V.   COMP. V.
            <u>Will</u> | <u>you</u> | <u>go</u> to the party with us or <u>stay</u> at home?

EXERCISE 3   Identifying Compound Subjects and Compound Verbs

In each of the sentences below, underline the subject once and the verb twice. Include all parts of a compound subject or a compound verb and all words in a verb phrase.

EX. 1. <u>Leon</u> and <u>Cesar</u> <u><u>butter</u></u> and <u><u>toast</u></u> their bread for breakfast.

1. As early as 2600 B.C., the Egyptians baked and toasted bread.

2. Toasting or roasting can remove mold and moisture from the bread.

3. In the eighteenth century, people in Great Britain and people in North America called two connected forks a toaster.

4. The fork toaster sandwiched the bread and toasted it over a fire.

5. Tin and wire formed a cage-shaped toaster in the nineteenth century.

6. This toaster held four slices of bread and sat over a coal stove.

7. At the turn of the century, with the invention of electric toasters, toast could finally be made and enjoyed without lighting a stove.

8. Toasters quickly became popular and were installed in kitchens and even in bedrooms.

9. In 1919, a mechanic invented the pop-up toaster and filed for a patent.

10. Springs and a timer were built into the new, automatic toaster.

EXERCISE 4   Using Compound Subjects and Compound Verbs to Combine Sentences

Combine each of the following groups of two or three short sentences into one longer sentence by using compound subjects or compound verbs. Write each new sentence on the line provided.

EX. 1. In the evening, Emily called to remind me about band practice.
Jason called to remind me about band practice, too.
In the evening, both Emily and Jason called to remind me about band practice.

1. The house painters scraped the wood-framed house. They also primed the house. Finally, they painted the house.

    _____

2. This summer, Mr. Ruffolo traveled by train to Canada. Mrs. Ruffolo rode the train to Canada, too.

    _____

3. After cleaning the garage, Lucas played basketball. Then he ate dinner. Finally, Lucas studied for his exam.

    _____

4. Grilled swordfish is especially tasty. Grilled salmon is tasty, too.

    _____

5. Mosi enjoys a game of chess. Eric and Julio enjoy playing chess, too.

    _____

6. After school yesterday, Nina met Felicia at the health food store. Rosa was also at the health food store.

    _____

7. Yesterday morning, Frank jogged two miles. Next, he ate breakfast. Then he showered and dressed for school.

    _____

8. Amanda wrote her first short story. She showed it to her friend Reese.

    _____

9. After skiing, Pearl removed her hat and gloves. She took off her boots. Then she warmed her feet by the fireplace.

    _____

10. After the art history lecture, Cora went to the library. Ben went to the library.

    _____

FINDING THE SUBJECT OF A SENTENCE

2f   To find the subject of a sentence, ask *Who?* or *What?* before the verb.

EXAMPLES   The **team** of doctors **worked** hard to save the patient. [Who worked? *Team* worked.]

Across the finish line **jumped** the winning **frog.** [What jumped? The *frog* jumped.]

(1) The subject of a sentence expressing a command or a request is always understood to be *you*, although *you* may not appear in the sentence.

EXAMPLES   Eat a balanced meal for good health. [Who is being told to eat? *You* eat.]

Please read me the directions again, Kim. [Who is being asked to read? *You* read.]

(2) The subject of a sentence never appears in a prepositional phrase.

EXAMPLES   A **flock** of birds flew above the tall pine trees. [What flew? *A flock* flew. *Birds* is the object of the preposition *of.*]

A **group** of friends gathered near the doorway. [Who gathered? *Group* gathered. *Friends* is the object of the preposition *of.*]

(3) The subject of a sentence expressing a question usually follows the verb or a part of the verb phrase.

EXAMPLES   **Is** the **cat sleeping** on top of the desk? [What is sleeping on top of the desk? The *cat* is.]

When **was Carolyn elected** president of the student council? [Who was elected? *Carolyn* was elected.]

Were your **friends** early? [Who was early? *Friends* were.]

(4) The word *there* or *here* is never the subject of a sentence.

In the following examples, the words *there* and *here* are used as adverbs telling *where*.

EXAMPLES   There are the four suitcases we want to take. [What is there? The *suitcases* are there.]

Here is your new video game. [What is here? The *game* is here.]

In the following example, the word *there* is used as an ***expletive***—a word that fills out the structure of a sentence but does not add to the meaning.

EXAMPLE   There are two reasons for the delay of the game. [What are? *Reasons* are.]

EXERCISE 5   Identifying Subjects and Verbs

In each of the sentences below, underline the subject once and the verb twice. Include all parts of a compound subject or a compound verb and all words in a verb phrase.

EX. 1. At an early age, <u>Pablo Picasso</u> <u>showed</u> unusual artistic talent.

1. The son of an art teacher, Picasso was born in Spain in 1881.

2. At the age of twenty, he traveled to Paris for the first time.

3. Picasso's early paintings show the influence of other painters and his mastery of traditional techniques.

4. Despite the early-twentieth century popularity of Fauvism, Picasso followed his own path and questioned standard art forms.

5. Picasso and Georges Braque rejected the formal use of shapes and tried to show three dimensions in their paintings.

6. Together, the two painters developed Analytical Cubism.

7. Throughout their experiments with form, both common and unusual colors appeared in their artwork.

8. Picasso often placed various objects in his paintings.

9. His collages sometimes included newspaper, string, or wire.

10. In 1917, Picasso's interest in Classicism and his later connection with the Surrealists led to more analytical works.

11. His series of paintings and drawings with unusual figures of dancers started emerging from his studio in 1923 and developed over the next ten years.

12. In the 1930s, bull-fighting subjects appeared in Picasso's paintings.

13. His most important work during that time is the large mural *Guernica*.

14. Painted in 1937, *Guernica* is nearly twenty-six feet long and expresses Picasso's personal response to the Spanish Civil War.

15. Frightening images remained part of Picasso's work through World War II.

DIRECT OBJECTS AND INDIRECT OBJECTS

2g   A *complement* is a word or a group of words that completes the meaning of a verb.

INCOMPLETE   Jose Rodríguez threw

  COMPLETE   Jose Rodríguez threw the **ball.**

Generally, a sentence includes at least one complement. However, some sentences contain only a subject and a verb.

                          S.   V.   V.
EXAMPLES   Knute sang.   Run! [The subject *you* is understood.]

Direct objects and indirect objects are two kinds of complements.

2h   A *direct object* is a word or group of words that receives the action of a verb or shows the result of the action. A direct object tells *whom* or *what* after a transitive verb.

EXAMPLES   Angelina met **Susan** and **me** at the library. [Met whom? *Susan* and *me*.]
            Ms. Campbell recited the **poem** from memory. [Recited what? *Poem*.]

NOTE   For emphasis, a direct object may come before a subject and a verb.

        EXAMPLE   What an excellent safety **record** the driver holds! [Holds what? *Record*.]

2i   An *indirect object* is a word or group of words that comes between a transitive verb and a direct object and tells *to whom* or *to what*, or *for whom* or *for what*, the action of the verb is done.

EXAMPLES   Mr. Jacobs showed our **class** slides of Albert Pinkham Ryder's paintings. [Showed to whom? *Class*.]
            Pedro gave the **shelter** his extra wool sweaters and pants. [Gave to what? *Shelter*.]

NOTE   Do not confuse an adverb for a complement. Also, do not mistake a word in a prepositional phrase for a complement.

EXAMPLES   Janet plays **well.** [The adverb *well* tells *how* Janet plays.]
            Janet plays **with the band.** [The noun *band* is the object of the preposition *with*.]

EXERCISE 6 Identifying Direct and Indirect Objects

Underline the direct objects once and indirect objects twice in each of the sentences below. [Note: Not every sentence has an indirect object.]

EX. 1. Jared fed his baby <u>brother</u> a <u>bottle</u> of milk.

1. The department gave Constance a surprise retirement party.
2. Lorenzo collected aluminum cans and plastic bottles for recycling.
3. Mrs. Duffy fed her roses the new plant food.
4. The engineer showed David and Mateo the design for the water system.
5. What a dramatic role the actor played!
6. The judge gave her a lenient sentence.
7. Sam demonstrated the new machinery to the production staff.
8. Aunt Sarah brought my sister and me a gift from her trip.
9. Melvin showed Ruben and Sally his notes on the political debate.
10. Brandon served the guests fresh sea bass and a salad.
11. Ramon and Maya built a front porch for their mother's house.
12. The architect showed the principal the plans for the school's new gym.
13. Emily's brilliant news articles won the magazine many awards.
14. The stranger gave us directions to the nearest museum.
15. Mr. Chan showed the students a slide show about early computers.

EXERCISE 7 Writing Direct Objects and Indirect Objects

On your own paper, finish the sentences below according to the guidelines. In your sentences, underline the direct objects once and the indirect objects twice.

EX. 1. Vera told _____. (*Add a direct and an indirect object.*)
    1. *Vera told <u>me</u> a <u>secret</u> about the new recreation center.*

1. Please give _____. (*Add a direct and an indirect object.*)
2. Stan read _____. (*Add a direct and an indirect object.*)
3. Do you know _____? (*Add a compound direct object.*)
4. Cassie suggested _____. (*Add a direct object.*)
5. She promised _____. (*Add a direct and an indirect object.*)
6. Tito wrote _____. (*Add a direct and an indirect object.*)
7. I understand _____. (*Add a direct object.*)
8. Ho handed _____. (*Add a direct and an indirect object.*)
9. Joel interviewed _____. (*Add a direct object.*)
10. We showed _____. (*Add a direct and an indirect object.*)

OBJECTIVE COMPLEMENTS

2j An *objective complement* is a word or group of words that helps complete the meaning of a transitive verb by identifying or modifying the direct object.

An objective complement may be a noun or an adjective. The complement may also be compound.

EXAMPLES   Eli and Joy named their son **Kai.**
                        Tony painted the fence **green** and **white.**

Only a few verbs take an objective complement: *consider, make*, and verbs that can be replaced by *consider* or *make*, such as *appoint, call, choose, elect, name, cut, paint*, and *sweep.*

EXERCISE 8   Identifying Objective Complements

Underline the objective complement in each of the sentences below.

   EX. 1. The contestants considered the questions <u>difficult</u>.

   1. The judge found the jury's decision surprising.

   2. The students elected Veronica treasurer.

   3. They named the new restaurant Pasta Pasta.

   4. Ben painted the kitchen walls blue.

   5. Nina made the shower invitations pink and silver.

   6. Herb swept the sidewalk clean.

   7. The neighborhood appointed Kim chairperson of the block party.

   8. Many student volunteers made the dance a success.

   9. Lena named her two dogs Holly and Chester.

   10. The salesperson called the hand cream miraculous.

   11. Tomás cut the puzzle pieces smaller.

   12. The summer rains made the islands green and lush.

   13. Everyone thinks him reliable.

   14. Jiro thought the exam simple.

   15. Katherine dyed the wool purple.

MODULE 2: THE SENTENCE

REVIEW EXERCISE

A. Identifying Complete Subjects and Verbs

For each sentence below, put brackets around the complete subject. Then underline the simple subject once and the verb twice. Be sure to include all parts of a compound subject or a compound verb.

EX. 1. [Antonia and Maria] visited their friends over summer break.

1. My friends Sylvia, Anna, and Felicia live in California.
2. The bus ride lasted many hours and exhausted Antonia and Maria.
3. The bus driver and the passengers stopped for meals in small towns.
4. Antonia and Maria had seats near the driver.
5. Arriving in San Franciso, Antonia and Maria saw their friends' waving hands and smiling faces.

B. Identifying Direct Objects, Indirect Objects, and Objective Complements

Identify the italicized complement in each of the following sentences. On the line before each sentence, write *d.o.* for *direct object, i.o.* for *indirect object*, or *obj. c.* for *objective complement.*

EX. *d.o.* 1. Mesopotamians invented the *umbrella* 3,400 years ago.

_____ 1. Early umbrellas protected *Mesopotamians* from the desert sun.

_____ 2. Even today, ancient traditions decide the *use* of the umbrella.

_____ 3. In many African societies, umbrella bearers protect *chiefs* from the sun.

_____ 4. The ancient Egyptians considered the umbrella *religious* and *heavenly.*

_____ 5. As a high honor, a leader might offer *someone* the umbrella.

_____ 6. Whether made of palm leaves, feathers, or stretched papyrus, the Egyptian umbrella and its shade symbolized royal *protection.*

_____ 7. The Greeks and Romans borrowed the *idea* of the umbrella from the Egyptians.

_____ 8. Greek women considered the white parasol a *status symbol.*

_____ 9. In the first century A.D., a Roman emperor gave *women* the right to protect themselves from the rain with umbrellas.

_____ 10. Roman women gave their paper *umbrellas* a coating of oil.

SUBJECT COMPLEMENTS

A *subject complement* is a word or word group that completes the meaning of a linking verb and identifies or modifies the subject.

2k A *predicate nominative* is the word or group of words that follows a linking verb and refers to the same person or thing as the subject of the verb.

EXAMPLES   Mary Cassatt was a famous impressionist **painter.** [The noun *painter* refers to the subject *Mary Cassatt.*]
Mrs. Fitzgerald was **one** of the school board candidates. [The pronoun *one* refers to the subject *Mrs. Fitzgerald.*]

2l A *predicate adjective* is an adjective that follows a linking verb and modifies the subject of the verb.

EXAMPLES   The autumn sky is **blustery.** [The adjective *blustery* modifies the subject *sky.*]
All of the contestants looked **nervous** but **excited.** [The adjectives *nervous* and *excited* modify the subject *All.*]

NOTE   A predicate nominative or a predicate adjective may be compound.

     EXAMPLES   The winners are **Adela** and **Luis.** [compound predicate nominative]
Our weather was **cold, rainy,** and **windy.** [compound predicate adjective]

EXERCISE 9   Identifying Linking Verbs and Subject Complements

In each of the following sentences, underline the subject complement once and the linking verb twice. On the line before the sentence, identify the complement by writing *p.n.* for *predicate nominative* or *p.a.* for *predicate adjective.*

     EX. _*p.a.*_   1. Last night the honking geese <u>sounded</u> <u>lonely</u>.

_____   1. Usually, autumn nights are quiet and calm.

_____   2. From my bedroom window, the trees look bent and craggy.

_____   3. In my backyard, the tree with the thick, black trunk is an oak.

_____   4. Of all the trees in our yard, the oak is the oldest one.

_____   5. Now all of the trees are bare.

_____   6. What a wonderful season autumn is!

_____ 7. The days grow shorter.

_____ 8. Cool temperatures and brisk winds feel refreshing.

_____ 9. An autumn moon can be golden and bright.

_____ 10. Of the four seasons, autumn appears the most colorful time to me.

_____ 11. Neighbors are busy with preparations for the cold weather.

_____ 12. Mulching trees and bushes is a necessary chore before the arrival of winter.

_____ 13. The bush with the bronze, drooping blossom heads is a hydrangea.

_____ 14. The hydrangea flowers remain bronze all through the winter.

_____ 15. Those striking flowers with the yellow petals and black centers are black-eyed Susans.

_____ 16. Both black-eyed Susans and bee balm are good sources of seeds for birds in winter.

_____ 17. Bee balm smells spicy.

_____ 18. After a frost, bee balm leaves become gray and brown.

_____ 19. In autumn, almost all of the flowers look scraggly and worn.

_____ 20. The season of renewal is spring.

EXERCISE 10   Writing Subject Complements

Complete each of the sentences below with the type of subject complement requested in parentheses. Write your answers on the lines provided.

EX. 1. The runners in the park are (*predicate adjective*) ____*energetic*____ .

1. My cousin Tita is (*predicate nominative*) _____ .

2. The trees are (*predicate adjective*) _____ .

3. The winners of the music scholarships are (*compound predicate nominative*)

   _____ .

4. All of the candidates look (*compound predicate adjective*) _____

   _____ .

5. The owner of the new home on Sierra Street is (*predicate nominative*)

   _____ .

CLASSIFICATION OF SENTENCES

Sentences may be classified according to purpose.

2m   A *declarative sentence* makes a statement. It is followed by a period.

EXAMPLES   George Washington was the first president of the United States.
The front tires on the car are flat, and I will have to fix them.

2n   An *interrogative sentence* asks a question. It is followed by a question mark.

EXAMPLES   Have you ever traveled to Colorado?
Do you like stir-fry made with vegetables and tofu?

2o   An *imperative sentence* makes a request or gives a command. It is usually followed by a period. A very strong command, however, is followed by an exclamation point.

EXAMPLES   Please give me the date of my dentist appointment.
Stop running!

2p   An *exclamatory sentence* expresses strong feeling or shows excitement. It is followed by an exclamation point.

EXAMPLES   What a motivating speech she gave!
Oh, you were hired for the job!

EXERCISE 11   Classifying the Four Kinds of Sentences

Classify each of the following sentences. On the line before each sentence, write *dec.* for *declarative, inter.* for *interrogative, imp.* for *imperative,* or *excl.* for *exclamatory.* Then add the appropriate end mark to each sentence.

EX. ___*imp.*___   1.   Please lend me your copy of *As You Like It.*

_____   1.   Have you finished your writing assignment

_____   2.   Call the paramedics—now

_____   3.   Fruits and vegetables are good for you, and you should eat two to four servings of each daily

_____   4.   Is Boston the capital of Massachusetts

_____   5.   What is your favorite movie

_____ 6. What an inspired leader she is

_____ 7. I've heard that downhill skiing can be an exciting and exhilarating sport, but it looks dangerous to me

_____ 8. Which do you enjoy more, Chinese food or Italian food

_____ 9. Please call Phoebe after school

_____ 10. Mr. DeSoto told me that repairing plaster walls can be difficult and time-consuming work

_____ 11. Help me

_____ 12. Have you ever traveled to Spain

_____ 13. Kim and Alex are the best artists in our class, but Ernesto has the most original ideas

_____ 14. What an amazing performance that was

_____ 15. Write your answers on a separate piece of paper

_____ 16. Oh, no, you've ruined the experiment

_____ 17. When did you publish your first story

_____ 18. Dogs can be loyal companions; however, they do require a good deal of care and attention

_____ 19. What did you eat for breakfast

_____ 20. Poor thing, you look absolutely exhausted

_____ 21. My friends will be arriving soon

_____ 22. How long is that scarf

_____ 23. Stop the show

_____ 24. Please give Jeremy the message as soon as he gets home from work

_____ 25. Oh, I'm late

EXERCISE 12   Writing Sentences

On your own paper, write ten sentences using each of the four types of sentences at least once. After each sentence, write _dec._ for _declarative, inter._ for _interrogative, imp._ for _imperative_, or _excl._ for _exclamatory_. Be sure to add the appropriate end mark to each sentence.

EX. 1. _Do you know the answer? (inter.)_

A. Identifying Subjects, Verbs, and Complements

On the line before each sentence below, identify the underlined word or word group by writing *s.* for *subject, v.* for *verb*, or *c.* for *complement*. Classify each complement by writing *d.o.* for *direct object, i.o.* for *indirect object, obj. c. for objective complement, p.n.* for *predicate nominative*, or *p.a.* for *predicate adjective*.

EX. __*c. (p.n.)*__   1.   The Marx Brothers were popular <u>comedians</u> on the stage, the screen, and the radio.

_____   1.   Famous for their inventive humor, the <u>Marx Brothers</u> made film versions of their stage comedies in the late 1920s.

_____   2.   *Duck Soup, Animal Crackers*, and *A Night at the Opera* are their best-known <u>pictures.</u>

_____   3.   Groucho Marx was a <u>master</u> of the wisecrack.

_____   4.   In his unpredictable style, Groucho often <u>strode</u> with bent knees across the stage floor.

_____   5.   In contrast to Groucho's busy actions, Harpo Marx calmly played <u>music</u> on the harp.

_____   6.   A third brother, Chico Marx, played the <u>piano</u> and even smashed it on one occasion.

_____   7.   All five of the original Marx brothers were <u>successful,</u> but Gummo Marx left the act.

_____   8.   During World War II, Chico became a band leader, and Zeppo was a theatrical <u>agent.</u>

_____   9.   Groucho Marx brought his <u>fans</u> much entertainment as the television quizmaster on *You Bet Your Life.*

_____   10.   Many years have passed since Julius Henry Marx named his memorable character <u>Groucho.</u>

B. Classifying Sentences

Identify each of the following sentences. On the line before each sentence, write *dec.* for *declarative, inter.* for *interrogative, imp.* for *imperative*, or *excl.* for *exclamatory*. Then add the appropriate end mark to each sentence.

EX. __*dec.*__ 1.   The raspberry bushes produced many berries this year

_____   1.   Please open the door for me

_____   2.   Why wasn't Marlene in school today

_____ 3. Tamisha wants to be a photographer

_____ 4. What an important scientific breakthrough this is

_____ 5. We cleaned the house before leaving for the movie

_____ 6. Visit the seashore's fine seafood restaurants and miles of beaches

_____ 7. Are you registering for the photography workshop

_____ 8. What a wonderful birthday

_____ 9. Is there a job opening for a cashier on weekends

_____ 10. The extended forecast calls for a chance of snow flurries on Wednesday

C. Writing Sentences

On your own paper, write one sentence according to each of the guidelines below. In your sentences, underline the words that indicate the italicized sentence parts. Also, use a variety of subjects, verbs, and complements in your sentences.

EX. 1. an interrogatory sentence with a compound indirect object

1. *Did you bring <u>Harry</u> and <u>Cora</u> their new books?*

1. a declarative sentence with a *compound subject*

2. an exclamatory sentence with a *direct object*

3. a declarative sentence with a *predicate nominative*

4. an interrogative sentence with a *compound predicate adjective*

5. an imperative sentence with an *indirect object*

6. an interrogative sentence with a *compound verb*

7. a declarative sentence with a *direct object*

8. an exclamatory sentence with an *indirect object*

9. an interrogative sentence with a *predicate nominative*

10. an imperative sentence with a *compound direct object*

11. an exclamatory sentence with a *predicate adjective*

12. a declarative sentence with an *indirect object and a direct object*

13. an imperative sentence with a *compound verb*

14. an interrogative sentence with a *compound direct object*

15. a declarative sentence with a *compound verb*

MODULE 3: THE PHRASE

PREPOSITIONAL PHRASES

3a   A *phrase* is a group of related words that is used as a single part of speech and does not contain both a verb and its subject.

3b   A *prepositional phrase* is a group of words consisting of a preposition, a noun or pronoun that serves as the *object of the preposition*, and any modifiers of that object.

EXAMPLES   The brick house **with the green shutters** is Jaime's home. [The noun *shutters* is the object of the preposition *with*.]
Behind it are a vegetable garden and raspberry bushes. [The pronoun *it* is the object of the preposition *Behind*.]

An object of a preposition may be compound.

EXAMPLE   **Near the garden and raspberry bushes,** wasps are building a nest. [Both *garden* and *bushes* are objects of the preposition *Near*.]

EXERCISE 1   Identifying Prepositional Phrases and Their Objects

Find the prepositional phrase in each of the following sentences. Underline the preposition once and the object of the preposition twice.

EX.   [1]   We drove <u>through</u> the <u>park</u> to see the ice skaters.

[1] Ice skaters swirled across the frozen pond. [2] Above them shone a bright moon and starry sky. [3] Spectators watched from the park benches. [4] Everyone was bundled in bulky, woolen layers. [5] Occasionally, a spectator went into the warming house. [6] Only the skaters, with their glowing faces, seemed oblivious of the cold. [7] Inside the warming house, a young park employee named Salvadore tended a crackling fire and served hot cider. [8] Pairs of skates were lined up by the hearth. [9] Salvadore stoked the fire and from the window longingly watched the skaters. [10] He was eager to join the other skaters and glide across the ice in his new skates. [11] Under his breath, he muttered something. [12] A few more spectators came through the door of the warming house. [13] One of the spectators stood beside Salvadore. [14] He was a tall, elderly gentleman wearing a bright red scarf around his neck. [15]

"Young man, why aren't you on the ice?" he asked Salvadore. [16] Salvadore explained that he was working but pointed to his skates underneath a bench. [17] After much discussion, Salvadore loaned the man his skates. [18] On the man's feet, the skates gleamed. [19] Thanking Salvadore, the man bowed and skated swiftly across the pond. [20] Salvadore smiled as his new friend twirled in front of the spectators, the tail of his bright red scarf waving behind him.

EXERCISE 2   Writing a Design Report

Write a description of your dream house for an architect. Remember to include bathrooms and closets. On your own paper, write ten sentences about your house. Include at least ten prepositional phrases. Underline each prepositional phrase that you use.

EX. 1. *A large closet for coats is to the right.*

3c An *adjective phrase* is a prepositional phrase that modifies a noun or a pronoun.

An adjective phrase tells *what kind* or *which one*. An adjective phrase always follows the word it modifies.

EXAMPLES   A glass **of iced tea** is refreshing. [The phrase modifies the noun *glass*, telling *what kind*.]
Her eyes looked like those **of her mother.** [The phrase modifies the pronoun *those*, telling *which ones*.]
The treasure **at the edge of the old graveyard** was never found. [The phrase *at the edge* modifies the noun *treasure*. *Edge* is the object of the preposition *at*. The phrase *of the old graveyard* modifies *edge*.]

3d An *adverb phrase* is a prepositional phrase that modifies a verb, an adjective, or an adverb.

An adverb phrase tells *how, when, where, why*, or *to what extent*.

EXAMPLES   The helicopter hovered **over the landing pad.** [The phrase modifies the verb *hovered*, telling *where*.]
Her clothing was black **with soot and mud.** [The phrase modifies the adjective *black*, telling *how*.]
We painted the house completely **except for the window trim.** [The phrase modifies the adverb *completely*, telling *to what extent*.]

An adverb phrase, unlike an adjective phrase, can precede the word it modifies.

EXAMPLE   **During his friend's stay,** Mr. Bruce slept **on the floor in a sleeping bag.** [Each phrase modifies the verb *slept. During his friend's stay* tells *when; on the floor* tells *where*; and *in a sleeping bag* tells *how*.]

More than one prepositional phrase can modify the same word.

EXAMPLE   The picture **of the author on the book jacket** is quite flattering. [Each phrase modifies the noun *picture*. Both *of the author* and *on the book jacket* tell *which one*.]

EXERCISE 3   Identifying Adjective and Adverb Phrases

In the sentences below, underline each adjective phrase once and each adverb phrase twice.

    EX. 1. The greatest number <u>of grasshoppers</u> live <u>in grasslands and semi-arid regions</u>.

1. Their colors range from green to brown.
2. Markings of red or yellow appear on some grasshoppers.
3. Organs for smell are located on a grasshopper's antennae.
4. Grasshoppers also have a sense of touch.
5. They have feelers on their heads, legs, and abdomens.
6. Grasshoppers actually leap through the air, although they do have wings.
7. Some grasshoppers lay their eggs on underwater plants.
8. The katydid is a type of grasshopper.
9. Katydids live on trees and in bushes or grasses.
10. Many species of katydid look like leaves.
11. Katydids are known as singers.
12. Locusts, which can devastate crops when they migrate in swarms, are also grasshoppers.
13. Locusts fly in the air in swarms when their body temperatures rise.
14. In 1889, a huge swarm was seen crossing the Red Sea.
15. Stopping a locust swarm in motion is nearly impossible.

EXERCISE 4   Revising Sentences Using Prepositional Phrases

For each of the sentences below, add a prepositional phrase as a modifier. Use at least five adjective phrases and five adverb phrases. Classify each phrase and underline the word each phrase modifies. Write your sentences on your own paper.

    EX. 1. The tree leaves fell.
        1. *The tree leaves <u>fell</u> in the yard. (adverb)*

1. The woman stepped quickly.
2. Is that your camera?
3. Let's go.
4. Do you still have salamanders?
5. I will send them an email.
6. The goats are loose!
7. "How many do you want?" Loretta asked.
8. That stuff is hers.
9. I love tomatoes.
10. The cat looks quite comfortable.

MODULE 3: THE PHRASE

PARTICIPLES AND PARTICIPIAL PHRASES

A *verbal* is a form of a verb used as a noun, an adjective, or an adverb. The three kinds of verbals are the *participle*, the *gerund*, and the *infinitive*.

A *verbal phrase* consists of a verbal and its modifiers and complements.

3e   A *participle* **is a verb form that is used as an adjective.**

There are two kinds of participles—the **present participle** and the **past participle.** The perfect tense of a participle is formed with a past participle and the helping verb *having*.

PRESENT   **Smiling,** the two sisters waved to the class. [*Smiling*, a form of the verb *smile*, modifies the noun *sisters*.]

Emilio heard something **rustling** outside the tent. [*Rustling*, a form of the verb *rustle*, modifies the pronoun *something*.]

PAST   The **grilled** catfish with lemon tasted delicious. [*Grilled*, a form of the verb *grill*, modifies the noun *catfish*.]

Thrilled and excited, they scrambled into the roller-coaster car. [*Thrilled*, a form of the verb *thrill*, and *excited*, a form of the verb *excite*, modify the pronoun *they*.]

PERFECT   **Having studied** all day, Jessica was ready for her test. [*Having studied*, a form of the verb *study*, modifies the noun *Jessica*.]

Having been soaked by the rain, the cat looked unhappy. [*Having been soaked*, a form of the verb *soak*, modifies the noun *cat*.]

3f   **A *participial phrase* consists of a participle and all of the words related to the participle.**

EXAMPLES   **Running along the lakefront,** a group of joggers stopped to watch the sunrise. [The participial phrase modifies the noun *group*. The adverb phrase *along the lakefront* modifies the present participle *Running*.]

Eduardo, **delighted immensely by the book,** lent it to his best friend. [The participial phrase modifies the noun *Eduardo*.]

EXERCISE 5   Identifying Participles and Participial Phrases

Underline the participles and participial phrases used as adjectives in the following sentences.

EX.   1. <u>Having cleaned her room</u>, Gemma went outside for a walk.

1. Allison, racing down the stairs, dropped her books.
2. Michael's father served baked chicken with wild rice and mushrooms.
3. Waiting for her ride to school, Marie saw a deer leap into the woods.
4. Having written a short story, Andrew asked Carmen to read it.
5. Tuned to perfection, the engine purred.
6. Finding herself alone in the house, Amanda turned up the radio.
7. The wooden floors, having been rubbed with oil, gleamed.
8. My brother and sister start their cooking lessons next week.
9. We could see shooting stars in the sky.
10. The group of friends, having dined together, sat and talked for hours.

EXERCISE 6   Identifying Participles and Participial Phrases and the Words They Modify

Underline once the participles and participial phrases in the following sentences. Then underline twice the word or words each participle or participial phrase modifies.

EX.   1. <u>Known as the "Iron Horse,"</u> <u>Lou Gehrig</u> was one of baseball's greatest hitters.

1. Basking in the audience's applause, Sara took a deep bow.

2. Named after a Bantu word for *okra*, gumbo is a spicy Creole stew.

3. Speaking eloquently, the First Lady captivated the senators.

4. The reward, announced in the newspaper, was a large sum of money.

5. The retriever, known for his gentle nature, played catch with the children.

6. Waving from the car, the O' Shea family left on vacation.

7. In your own words, explain each concept presented in the first module.

8. The potluck dinner, grilled chicken and steamed corn, tasted surprisingly good.

9. Having measured and marked the wood, the carpenter began to saw.

10. We heard something tapping on the window.

11. Someone's cell phone, beeping loudly, alarmed the cockatiel.

12. Can you find the creatures hidden in this picture puzzle?

13. The Parthenon, visited by tourists and scholars, overlooks the city of Athens, Greece.

14. Living on a farm, I always have something to do.

15. My father, writing a book on cacti, teaches in the botany department.

GERUNDS AND GERUND PHRASES

3g   **A *gerund* is a verb form ending in –*ing* that is used as a noun.**

Like nouns, gerunds can be subjects, predicate nominatives, direct objects, or objects of prepositions.

EXAMPLES   **Yodeling** is my favorite type of music. [subject]
    One good aerobic sport is **skating**. [predicate nominative]
    I do not like **collecting** stamps as much as I used to. [direct object]
    In school we heard a lecture on **voting**. [object of a preposition]

Do not confuse a gerund with a present participle used as part of a verb phrase or as an adjective.

GERUND   The teachers have finished **eating** lunch. [*Eating* is the direct object of the verb *have finished*.]

PRESENT PARTICIPLES   The teachers **are** still **eating** lunch. [*Eating* is part of the verb phrase *are eating*.]

    The teachers **eating** lunch will finish soon. [*Eating* is used as an adjective to modify the noun *teachers*.]

3h   **A *gerund phrase* consists of a gerund and any modifiers and complements it may have. The entire gerund phrase acts as a noun.**

Like gerunds, gerund phrases can be subjects, predicate nominatives, direct objects, or objects of prepositions.

EXAMPLES   **Walking in deep sand** is good for your feet. [The phrase is the subject of the sentence.]
    His problem now was **getting the part back into the box**. [The phrase is a predicate nominative.]
    I really like **riding my skateboard fast**. [The phrase is the object of the verb *like*.]
    You don't need binoculars for **birdwatching from Terry's house**. [The phrase is the object of the preposition *for*.]

NOTE   When a noun or a pronoun comes immediately before a gerund, it is in the possessive form and is considered part of the gerund phrase.

EXAMPLES   **Demi's whistling** woke the baby.
    When he's awake, the baby likes **her whistling**.

EXERCISE 7   Identifying Gerunds and Gerund Phrases and Their Uses

Underline the gerunds or gerund phrases in the sentences below. Then on the line before each sentence, identify how each gerund or gerund phrase is used by writing *s.* for *subject*, *p.n.* for *predicate nominative*, *d.o.* for *direct object*, or *o.p.* for *object of a preposition*.

EX. _____*o.p.*_____ 1. I feel like <u>washing the windows today</u>.

_____ 1. Some people deal with their feelings by talking about them.

_____ 2. Sweeping that barn will take some time.

_____ 3. I don't like being here any more than you do.

_____ 4. Much effort goes into throwing a good party.

_____ 5. "How do you like using your new desk, Jo?"

_____ 6. I'd advise wearing a sweater when you go.

_____ 7. Mom got a ticket for running a red light.

_____ 8. Suturing the incision is one of the last steps in surgery.

_____ 9. The choir was going to the meeting hall for singing and ice cream.

_____ 10. The tar's sticking to Zoe's shoe posed a problem.

_____ 11. Printing was invented in Europe in the 1450s.

_____ 12. I like collecting shells and cataloging them.

_____ 13. Do you enjoy working at the clinic?

_____ 14. Reading the newspaper is a daily activity for me.

_____ 15. The pioneer family's dream was owning their own farmland.

_____ 16. He signaled by raising his right hand.

_____ 17. Estimating the number of beans in the jar is almost impossible.

_____ 18. The problem is getting someone to donate furniture for the play.

_____ 19. Phyllis always makes time for reading to the kindergarten class.

_____ 20. There is a renewed interest in raising funds for a new gym.

3i   An *infinitive* is a verb form that can be used as a noun, an adjective, or an adverb. An infinitive usually begins with *to*.

NOUN   **To act** on stage is Melissa's dream.

ADJECTIVE   Her first attempt **to act** was a success.

ADVERB   Finally, Melissa moved to New York **to act.**

The word *to*, the sign of the infinitive, is sometimes omitted.

EXAMPLES   Let them [to] **eat** cake.
Make them all [to] **wash** their hands.
You ought not [to] **stand** like that.

3j   An *infinitive phrase* consists of an infinitive and all of the words related to the infinitive.

EXAMPLES   Rebecca plans **to move to another neighborhood soon.**
Because of the barking dogs, Lisa was unable **to finish the module.**

NOTE   Unlike other verbals, an infinitive may have a subject. Such a construction is called an *infinitive clause.*

EXAMPLE   Luc wanted **Enzo to pour the milk.** [*Enzo* is the subject of the infinitive *to pour*. The entire infinitive clause is the direct object of the verb *wanted*.]

EXERCISE 8   Identifying Infinitives

Underline the infinitives in the following paragraph.

EX.   [1] <u>To learn</u> and <u>to understand</u> Italian cooking, read Marcella Hazan's cookbooks.

[1] In her cookbook's introduction, Ms. Hazan writes that simple, satisfying food has only one objective: to taste good. [2] This cookbook, *Marcella's Italian Kitchen*, lists a few "elementary rules" to teach the basics of making Italian food. [3] Use no other oil but olive oil to dress salads. [4] Grate fresh cheese when you are ready to use it. [5] Other introductory notes teach how to choose and to store olive oil. [6] To have the fresh and vital taste of an Italian dish, fresh tomatoes are required. [7] Ms. Hazan

asks us never to forget the fresh, ripe tomato. [8] To keep tomatoes fresh in winter, hang them in clusters on the vine in an airy, cool, dry place. [9] To compose an Italian menu, begin the meal with a soup or pasta, followed by fish or meat and a vegetable, and then a salad. [10] Some food can be prepared ahead of time, but plan to spend time in the kitchen just before the meal.

EXERCISE 9 Identifying Infinitive Phrases Used as Adjectives and Adverbs

Underline the infinitive phrases in the sentences below. Then, on the line before each sentence, write *adj.* if the phrase is used as an adjective or *adv.* if it is used as an adverb. Circle the word the phrase modifies.

EX. __*adv.*__ 1. Janet searched her closet to find the missing button.

_____ 1. With his friend Carlos, Juan helped Frank to paint his house.
_____ 2. The person to ask for advice is your mother.
_____ 3. Was Hannah's attempt to grow asparagus a success?
_____ 4. Dad made me sort the recyclables before I could go to play basketball.
_____ 5. With their friends, Vanessa and Kim went to the park to ski.
_____ 6. Fritz said, "I doubt I'll live to see the day you beat Nashota in tennis."
_____ 7. The Bears is the team to watch this year.
_____ 8. To play goalie, I need a different stick.
_____ 9. Trulia has a plan to revive the Yellow Knights.
_____ 10. The ship offloaded in Bangkok to make room for passengers.

EXERCISE 10 Identifying and Classifying Infinitive Phrases and Infinitive Clauses Used as Nouns

Underline the infinitive phrases and infinitive clauses in the sentences below. Then, on the line before each sentence, identify the function of each phrase by writing *s.* for *subject*, *d.o.* for *direct object*, or *p.n.* for *predicate nominative*.

EX. __*d.o.*__ 1. I've always wanted to play bagpipes.

_____ 1. Julio's brother reminded him to drive carefully in the rain.

_____ 2. To pick apples is a special pleasure on an autumn afternoon.

_____ 3. The office manager wanted Mario to apply for the new position.

_____ 4. Kwok often asks his grandfather to tell a story.

_____ 5. Alice's dream is to write a book about her grandmother.

A.   Identifying Adjective and Adverb Phrases

In the sentences below, classify each italicized phrase. On the line before the sentence, write *adj. phr.* for *adjective phrase* or *adv. phr.* for *adverb phrase*.

EX. *adj. phr.*   1.   The child *in the sunbonnet* played on the beach.

_____   1.   Visiting our classroom, the dentist gave a lecture *about oral hygiene.*

_____   2.   On horseback, the rangers rode along the border *between Mexico and Texas.*

_____   3.   The cardinals flocked *to the special sunflower feeder.*

_____   4.   We attended the pep rally *after school.*

_____   5.   Enjoying her trip to the museum, Andrea hid *behind the marble sarcophagus.*

_____   6.   The neighbors *down the block* play polka music all day long.

_____   7.   *With its long, slinky body*, the snake slithered its way across the short grass.

_____   8.   *After deliberating for days*, the jury reached a decision.

_____   9.   At our favorite Chinese restaurant, Randall ordered chicken *with peanuts and hot pepper sauce.*

_____   10.   Trying to get Andy's attention, Jeremy yelled *across the room.*

B.   Identifying Participial, Gerund, and Infinitive Phrases

On the line before each of the following sentences, identify the italicized phrase by writing *part. phr.* for *participial phrase, ger. phr.* for *gerund phrase*, or *inf. phr.* for *infinitive phrase.*

EX. *ger. phr.*   1.   By *gathering the suspects together*, the detective heightened the suspense.

_____   1.   *Swimming laps early in the morning* keeps me fit.

_____   2.   *To stop the river from overflowing*, volunteers placed thousands of sandbags along the banks.

_____   3.   *Nodding his head*, the student answered without speaking.

_____   4.   *Sipping a cup of hot jasmine tea* usually relaxes me in the evening.

_____   5.   The dog, *having been lost for a week*, looked shabby, hungry, and completely exhausted.

_____ 6. You'd better get down if you don't want *to fall from there*.

_____ 7. After *breaking the car window*, the emergency rescue team pulled Vlad from the wreck.

_____ 8. Mona listened carefully, *tuning the string* to the exact pitch.

_____ 9. "How did you enjoy *seeing <u>The Nutcracker</u>*, Kishi?"

_____ 10. Where there is smoke, there is not always fire *blazing out of control*.

C.   Using Phrases to Combine Sentences

Combine each group of sentences below into one sentence by changing the italicized sentence into a participial, a gerund, or an infinitive phrase. Use the hints in parentheses to help you. Write the new sentences on your own paper.

EX.   1. Tamara wanted to go to the beach. *She finished her finals on Tuesday.* (participle)

   1. *Finishing her finals on Tuesday, Tamara wanted to go to the beach.*

1. Robin hiked through part of the Sierra Nevada National Forest. *She stopped at Isabella Lake.* (participle)

2. *She discovered that she is allergic to eggs.* Now she makes salads for breakfast. (participle)

3. Caroline and Jack arrived early for the party. *They helped decorate.* (infinitive)

4. My friend Sheila writes poetry. *She began this while she was still in high school.* (gerund)

5. Cats see well in dim light. *They prowl and hunt at twilight.* (participle)

6. Marvella looked for a paper clip. *She had used the last staple.* (participle)

7. The church group sold homemade sandwiches. *The group was raising money.* (infinitive)

8. J. D. and Phoebe visited an island for their anniversary. *The island lies in the Caribbean Sea.* (participle)

9. The car had a flat tire. *It sat in the parking lot.* (participle)

10. Warren went to the mall. *He bought new shoes.* (infinitive)

APPOSITIVES AND APPOSITIVE PHRASES

3k   An *appositive* is a noun or a pronoun placed beside another noun or pronoun to identify or explain it.

EXAMPLES   Kimiko visited with her, the next-door **neighbor.** [The noun *neighbor* identifies the pronoun *her*.]
Sam Begay, my **neighbor** and best **friend**, won a scholarship to Arizona State University. [The nouns *neighbor* and *friend* explain the noun *Sam Begay*.]

3l   An *appositive phrase* consists of an appositive and its modifiers.

EXAMPLES   Those library books, **the ones that are overdue,** are mine.
For dinner we ate garden-fresh tomatoes and corn on the cob, **two of Armando's favorite foods**.

NOTE   An appositive usually follows the word it identifies or explains. For emphasis, however, an appositive may come at the beginning of a sentence.

   EXAMPLES   Miguel, **the winner of the award,** thanked his parents. [The noun *winner* refers to the noun *Miguel*.]

   An African American frontiersman, James Beckwourth discovered an important route through the Sierra Nevada mountains. [The noun *frontiersman* explains the noun *James Beckwourth*.]

EXERCISE 11   Identifying Appositives

Underline the appositive in each sentence. Then double underline the word or words the appositive identifies or explains.

   EX.   1. Those garden <u>tools</u>, the <u>ones</u> near the shed, are Mary's.

   1. My friends Mary and Hector are helping me plant bulbs and bushes.
   2. Hector's wheelbarrow, the one that is bright green, will carry a full load of compost.
   3. Yesterday we tilled the back border, the location for the peony bushes.
   4. Lemi's favorite flowers, peonies and daffodils, are my favorite flowers, too.
   5. Hector, an expert on peonies, has brought me many new varieties.
   6. We'll place the boldest colors, magenta and purple, near the porch steps.
   7. Whites and pinks, the most subdued colors, we'll place along the border.
   8. "Jack Snipe," a variety of narcissus, will surround the peonies in clusters.

9. In March and April, the months for early bloomers, bright yellow daffodil heads will pop up from the soil.

10. Mary and Hector, fellow enthusiasts of spring, are calling for my help.

EXERCISE 12   Identifying Appositive Phrases

Underline the appositive phrase in each sentence. Then double underline the word or words the appositive phrase identifies or explains.

EX.   1. Student Council is holding its next meeting on <u>January 3</u>, <u>the first day after winter break</u>.

1. Hail, ice pellets the size of walnuts, dented the car hood.

2. These fabrics, Egyptian cotton and linen, are cool and comfortable.

3. A translator fluent in five languages, Julia loves her career at the United Nations.

4. A young Pueblo potter, Diego shows a deep understanding of the generations of pottery tradition that have preceded him.

5. At the folk art exhibition we saw many traditional quilt patterns—Flying Geese, Log Cabin, and Dutch Mill.

6. Angela's sisters, owners of a clothing store, hired her to work part time after school.

7. The children were thrilled with the surprise, a calico kitten.

8. Deeply engrossed in a book, Manuel jumped when he heard the knock, a sharp rap on his door.

9. Derek's brother, a two-month-old baby, sleeps most of the time.

10. We gazed in wonder at the snow, a glittering blanket of white.

11. The biggest cow of the lot, the hungry one, is now eating happily.

12. If you are allergic to goldenrod, those tall weeds with yellow flowers, then you'd better stay away from my back yard.

13. I like adobe, that clay used in the Southwest to make houses, mostly because of its color.

14. Did you vote in the election yesterday, the one to choose the commencement speakers?

15. A magazine that comes with our Sunday paper, *Parade* has interesting articles.

MODULE REVIEW

A.   Identifying Adjective and Adverb Phrases

On the line before each sentence below, identify each italicized phrase by writing *adj. phr.* for *adjective phrase* or *adv. phr.* for *adverb phrase*.

EX. <u>*adj. phr.*</u>   1.   The almond tree *in front of the window* bloomed all spring.

_____   1.   Early *in the morning*, the courier delivered an urgent package.

_____   2.   The musicians *in the orchestra pit* had already tuned their instruments.

_____   3.   Having a map *of the museum* would be helpful.

_____   4.   In a blur, the cyclist flew *around the corner*.

_____   5.   They discovered his will *in a brittle, old book*.

_____   6.   *Before the huge audience*, Mildred delivered her lines gracefully.

_____   7.   The pair of shoes *under the bed* belongs to Joel.

_____   8.   *After the game* I'll have to finish my college application.

_____   9.   My checking account *at the bank* was closed.

_____   10.   I was *in your garage* fixing your car when the power went out.

B.   Identifying Verbal Phrases and Their Functions

On the line before each of the following sentences, identify each italicized phrase by writing *part. phr.* for *participial phrase*, *ger. phr.* for *gerund phrase*, or *inf. phr.* for *infinitive phrase*. Then identify the function of each phrase by writing *s.* for *subject*, *d.o.* for *direct object*, *i.o.* for *indirect object*, *p.n.* for *predicate nominative*, *adj.* for *adjective*, or *adv.* for *adverb*.

EX. <u>*part. phr.–adj.*</u>   1. Kuri heard something *tapping against the window*.

_____   1.   *Having heard the noise, too*, Kuri's brother Yoshi went to the window.

_____   2.   With her brother, Kuri went outside *to look around*.

_____   3.   A good way to deal with fear is *facing the fear directly*.

_____   4.   *Sitting there listening*, she had many unpleasant thoughts.

_____   5.   *Investigating the noise* required all their courage.

_____   6.   *Having gone outside*, Kuri and Yoshi discovered the cause of their scary noise.

_____ 7. The noise was coming from a branch *scraping against the house.*

_____ 8. *Solving the mystery* gave them some relief.

_____ 9. They decided *to return to the house.*

_____ 10. They postponed *cutting off the branch until the next morning.*

C. Writing Sentences with Phrases

On your own paper, write ten sentences according to the following guidelines. In each of your sentences, underline the italicized phrase given.

EX. 1. Use *lost under the porch* as a participial phrase.
1. *The kitten, <u>lost under the porch</u>, began to meow.*

1. Use *humming quietly* as a participial phrase.

2. Use *down the winding road* as an adverb phrase modifying a verb.

3. Use *jogging regularly* as a gerund phrase.

4. Use *to protect the houses* as an infinitive phrase used as a modifier.

5. Use *about her trip* as an adjective phrase.

6. Use *with fresh ingredients* as an adverb phrase modifying an adjective.

7. Use *of apples and oranges* as an adjective phrase.

8. Use *listening to the music* as a participial phrase.

9. Use *to be healthy* as an infinitive phrase used as a noun.

10. Use *a wonderful speaker* as an appositive phrase.

11. Use *disappearing into the fog* as a gerund phrase.

12. Use *to fill the barn with hay* as a modifier.

13. Use *working on the motor* as a gerund phrase.

14. Use *a sleek, shiny car* as an appositive.

15. Use *away from the wasps* as an adverb phrase.

MODULE 4: THE CLAUSE
KINDS OF CLAUSES

4a An *independent* (or *main*) *clause* expresses a complete thought and can stand by itself as a sentence.

EXAMPLES   **Geoffrey bought a pair of jeans**. [one independent clause]
Malcolm turned on the music and **Juanita adjusted the volume**. [two independent clauses joined by *and*]
Many companies are hiring part-time workers; these workers often do not have health insurance. [two independent clauses joined by a semicolon]
It rained all day after the storm arrived. [one independent clause combined with a subordinate clause]

4b A *subordinate* (or *dependent*) *clause* does not express a complete thought and cannot stand alone as a sentence.

Words such as *because, that*, or *whom* usually signal the beginning of a subordinate clause.

EXAMPLES   **because** they fixed the furnace
that danced the jitterbug
whom I saw on the roof

Subordinate means less important. The meaning of a subordinate clause is complete only when the clause is attached to an independent clause.

EXAMPLES   **Because they fixed the furnace,** we didn't have to replace it.
I hope the couple **who danced the jitterbug** wins the contest.
Do you know **whom I saw on the roof?**

As the preceding examples show, subordinate clauses can be located at the beginning, in the middle, or at the end of a sentence.

EXERCISE 1   Classifying Independent and Subordinate Clauses

In each of the following sentences, classify the italicized clause as independent or subordinate. On the line before each sentence, write *indep.* for *independent* or *sub.* for *subordinate*.

EX.   *sub.*   1. *Because Harry borrowed the car*, we drove to the dance.

_____   1. The newspaper article listed the hours of the recycling center, *which opens next Monday.*

_____ 2. *Emilio bought a leather saddle* for a low price at the flea market.

_____ 3. *After they left the movie*, they decided to stop for spring rolls and tea.

_____ 4. My Zeus, *whose bark is deep and loud*, just loves to cuddle and play.

_____ 5. *Kwok made the loaf of millet bread* that is sitting on the counter.

_____ 6. I hope the woman *who played the Schubert piece* wins the piano competition.

_____ 7. Amanda filled the tub with warm water, and *Jerry lifted the dog into the bath*.

_____ 8. *At first the number of ripe tomatoes in the kitchen was overwhelming*, but now I have several jars of canned tomatoes, paste, and sauce.

_____ 9. *Many Americans believe there is a need for health care reform*, which could make health care more affordable.

_____ 10. The panel of speakers answered several questions about international trade *after introductory comments were made*.

_____ 11. Paco was very upset when he saw that the boots, *which he had just bought*, had been left in the rain.

_____ 12. Leah put the bouquet of flowers on the table, and *Mark filled the water glasses*.

_____ 13. *After the recording session was over*, the musicians stayed in the studio for two hours.

_____ 14. *Some people freely give advice*, but seldom do they take it.

_____ 15. Do you know *what the Martinos named their baby daughter*?

_____ 16. The chef demonstrated *how he makes the dressing for the salad*.

_____ 17. *Mr. Thompson explained the safety-drill process*, repeating a few points for extra emphasis.

_____ 18. *When Linda mulched the leaves with the lawnmower*, she asked a neighbor to help.

_____ 19. The breakfast waffles, *which are made with sunflower seeds and pumpkin*, are Sara's specialty.

_____ 20. After Sharon read her essay to the class, *the students clapped*.

THE ADJECTIVE CLAUSE

4c **An *adjective clause* is a subordinate clause that modifies a noun or a pronoun.**

An adjective clause follows the word or words it modifies and tells *which one* or *what kind.* An adjective clause is usually introduced by a **relative pronoun.** The relative pronoun relates the clause to the word or words that the clause modifies.

Relative Pronouns				
that	which	who	whom	whose

EXAMPLES   Any traveler **who wants to reenter the country** needs a passport. [The clause modifies the noun *traveler*, telling *which one.*]
Kristina's Kitchen, **which serves the best hot cider,** is the place to go to warm up. [The clause modifies the noun phrase *Kristina's Kitchen*, telling *what kind* of restaurant.]

Sometimes the relative pronoun may be left out, but its meaning should be understood.

EXAMPLES   I'll never forget the robins **[that] we used to feed.**
Do you remember the time **[when] we went to Dodger Stadium**?

The relative adverbs *where* and *when* are sometimes used in adjective clauses.

EXAMPLES   That is the place **where the first owner is buried.**
My sister told me about the time **when she piloted an airplane.**

Depending on how it is used, an adjective clause is either essential or nonessential. An ***essential clause*** provides information that is necessary to the meaning of a sentence. A ***nonessential clause*** provides additional information that can be omitted without changing the meaning of a sentence. A nonessential clause is always set off by commas.

ESSENTIAL   Swimmers **who have entered the competition** should be in the gymnasium in one hour. [Omitting the adjective clause would change the meaning of the sentence.]

NONESSENTIAL   Sergei, **whose uncle is a composer,** plays the oboe. [The adjective clause gives extra information. Omitting the clause would not affect the meaning of the sentence.]

EXERCISE 2   Identifying Adjective Clauses and the Words Modified

In each sentence below, underline the adjective clause once and the relative pronoun or relative adverb twice. Then circle the word that the clause modifies.

EX. 1. In 1877, (Chief Joseph), who said, "I will fight no more forever," led the Nez Perce on a dramatic flight to Canada.

1. On the Ara River in Japan sits the city of Chichibu, which is known for its annual Shinto shrine festival.

2. I have seen nearly every film that this Italian director has made.

3. Our friends told us about the year when they hiked the Pacific Coast Trail.

4. From 2006 to 2010, our family lived in Texas, where our parents worked for the military.

5. I'm encouraged by volunteers who donate their time and effort.

6. Portugal is a country that I would enjoy visiting.

7. Last night we made a pasta sauce that included artichokes, calamata olives, and tomatoes.

8. Tomás's address book, which was bound in red leather, was nearly full.

9. Is there someone whom I can beat at tennis?

10. The photograph that Alfredo took was the only one taken of his grandfather.

EXERCISE 3   Revising Sentences by Using Adjective Clauses

Revise each of the sentences below by adding an adjective clause to modify the italicized noun. Write the revised sentences on your own paper. Use a variety of relative pronouns and relative adverbs to introduce your adjective clauses.

EX. 1. Helen finally found her *wallet*.
     1. *Helen finally found her wallet, which she misplaced last week.*

1. After school, Franklin went to the grocery *store*.

2. The broiled *salmon* tasted delicious.

3. The *fans* supported the team.

4. Somehow, Juanita heard about the surprise birthday *party*.

5. The student council *president* called the meeting to order.

THE ADVERB CLAUSE

4d **An *adverb clause* is a subordinate clause that modifies a verb, an adjective, or an adverb.**

An adverb clause tells *how, when, where, why, to what extent*, or *under what condition*.

EXAMPLES   Her face looked paler **than it had looked a moment before**. [The clause modifies the adjective *paler*. It tells *to what extent* her face looked pale.]
You may miss the show **if you eat dinner very late**. [The clause modifies the verb *have*. It tells *under what conditions* you may miss the show.]

An adverb clause that introduces a sentence is set off by a comma.

EXAMPLE   **As soon as you're through,** I'm leaving.

Common Subordinating Conjunctions			
after	as though	since	when
although	because	so that	whenever
as	before	than	where
as if	how	though	wherever
as long as	if	unless	whether
as soon as	in order that	until	while

NOTE   Some subordinating conjunctions may also be used as prepositions.

4e **Part of a clause may be omitted when the meaning can be understood from the context of the sentence. A clause with such an omission is called an *elliptical clause*.**

EXAMPLES   Brenda likes me better **than [she likes] him**.
When [he is] walking, he whistles patriotic tunes.

EXERCISE 4   Identifying Adverb Clauses and the Words They Modify

In the following sentences, underline each adverb clause once and the word or words it modifies twice.

EX.   1. Thomas <u>took</u> his first chess lesson <u>when he was six years old</u>.

1. Marie will call Patrick as soon as she knows the concert date.

2. The Falcons could win the game if they have a strong second half.

3. We changed our practice time because evening comes an hour earlier.

4. If we start now, we can avoid the seasonal shopping rush.

5. When away on a fishing trip, they call home every night.

6. Wherever they go, Mark and Kathleen take their two children.

7. Aunt Hazel lived with Alex and Kevin until her hip healed.

8. At first, speaking Spanish was embarrassing because I made mistakes.

9. If I eat an apple now, I won't eat popcorn at the movie.

10. Sondra will loan Marta her new dress tonight as long as Marta promises to return it on Sunday.

11. Whenever Ed visits, we drive to the peninsula and fish.

12. After the bolts came loose, the window shutters fell off the house.

13. Mr. Tomasini recycles more materials than anyone else in the neighborhood.

14. Before you leave, come to my office.

15. The young actress felt as though the bright lights were blinding her.

EXERCISE 5   Building Sentences With Adverb Clauses

On your own paper, write ten sentences that each contain an adverb clause. To create your sentences, join two clauses from the list below with a subordinating conjunction. Do not use any subordinating conjunction twice. Underline the adverb clauses in your sentences once and the subordinating conjunctions twice.

EX.   1.   the sun was shining; the children played outside
     1.   *Because the sun was shining*, the children played outside.

the baby was asleep	I help him
the storm arrives tonight	Lana thought of her friends
the papers are signed	she whispered softly
someone surprised him	the panel will discuss the issue
Juan solves math problems quickly	the deal is complete
the topic is interesting	it is protected in a glass case
she was traveling	we'll be snowed in tomorrow
the pottery vase is old	he jumped out of his chair

THE NOUN CLAUSE

4f   A *noun clause* is a subordinate clause used as a noun.

A noun clause may be used as a subject, a predicate nominative, a direct object, an indirect object, or an object of a preposition.

SUBJECT	**What Lani told me** helped me a great deal. [The clause is the subject of the verb *helped*.]
PREDICATE NOMINATIVE	That is **where I'd like to be.** [The clause follows the linking verb *is* and identifies the subject *That*.]
DIRECT OBJECT	Louis told us **why he was excited.** [The clause is the direct object of the verb *told*. It tells *what* Louis told.]
INDIRECT OBJECT	Jasper told **whoever would listen** the same story about his pet turtle. [The clause is the indirect object of the verb *told*. It tells *to whom* Jasper told the story.]
OBJECT OF A PREPOSITION	Did they give the food to **whoever asked for it?** [The clause is the object of the preposition *to*.]

Common Introductory Words for Noun Clauses		
how	when	who
if	where	whoever
that	whether	whom
what	which	whomever
whatever	whichever	why

Sometimes the introductory word in a noun clause is omitted.

EXAMPLE   She said **[that] her cold had cleared up**.

EXERCISE 6   Identifying and Classifying Noun Clauses

Underline the noun clause in each of the following sentences. On the line before the sentence, identify how the clause is used. Write *s.* for *subject*, *p.n.* for *predicate nominative*, *d.o.* for *direct object*, *i.o.* for *indirect object*, or *o.p.* for *object of a preposition*.

EX.   *p.n.*   1. That is <u>why I'm always a bit skeptical</u>.

_____   1. Joy told me that she was nervous.

_____ 2. Ms. Asato, a scientist, explained what ozone depletion is.

_____ 3. A motivated captain is what we need for this team.

_____ 4. The Little League coach will give whoever can throw farthest a position in the outfield.

_____ 5. Mrs. Castillo makes seafood paella for whoever asks.

_____ 6. Late for school, Mateo put on whichever shirt was nearest.

_____ 7. Do you know who created the sculpture known as *The Thinker*?

_____ 8. The small country's recently elected leader will announce what the new rationing laws are.

_____ 9. That we need rain is very evident.

_____ 10. The lawyer listened intently to whatever the witness said.

Writing Sentences with Noun Clauses

Write two sentences using each clause below as the two different parts of speech named in parentheses. Underline and label the use of each of the noun clauses. Write your sentences on your own paper.

EX. 1. that Ramon is going to the carnival tonight (*direct object; subject*)

1. that Stefano is going to play point guard for the basketball team (*direct object; predicate nominative*)

2. what Sondra made for lunch (*subject; object of a preposition*)

3. who announced the contest winners (*subject; predicate nominative*)

4. how they can plant saplings in their yards (*direct object; object of a preposition*)

5. whichever color you like best (*subject; object of a preposition*)

6. whatever she builds (*subject; indirect object*)

7. whoever returns the defective toaster (*indirect object; object of a preposition*)

8. whoever is working today (*indirect object; predicate nominative*)

9. where the sun shines year-round (*object of a preposition; direct object*)

10. why Uncle Jules didn't visit at Thanksgiving this year (*direct object; predicate nominative*)

SENTENCE STRUCTURE

The *structure* of a sentence is determined by the number of independent and subordinate clauses it contains.

4g   According to their structure, sentences are classified as *simple, compound, complex,* or *compound-complex*.

(1) A *simple sentence* has one independent clause and no subordinate clauses.

EXAMPLES   Uncle Harold threw me into the pool.
I would love to find an evening dress covered with sequins.
Should I go to the prom with Esteban?

(2) A *compound sentence* has two or more independent clauses but no subordinate clauses.

A compound sentence may be joined by a comma and a coordinating conjunction (*and, but, for, nor, or, so,* or *yet*); by a semicolon; or by a semicolon and a conjunctive adverb (*also, anyway, instead, still, therefore*) or a transitional expression (*as a result, in fact, for example*).

EXAMPLES   I went out for milk**, but** the store had already closed.
The rocking horse gathered dust in the attic**;** once it had been her favorite friend.
I do not really enjoy riding the bus**; however,** it is much cheaper than taking a taxi**; also,** it is faster than walking.

(3) A *complex sentence* has one independent clause and at least one subordinate clause.

EXAMPLES   Can you believe that I remembered your birthday!
President Carter, after he left office, helped build houses for the homeless.

(4) A *compound-complex* sentence has two or more independent clauses and at least one subordinate clause.

EXAMPLES   Isabel, who delivers our newspaper, often comes late, but she never apologizes for it.
Although we enjoy sweets, we avoid eating them, and we try to have fruit for dessert; sometimes we do not have dessert at all.

EXERCISE 8   Classifying Sentences According to Structure

Identify the structure of each of the sentences below. On the line before each sentence, write *simp.* for *simple, comp.* for *compound, cx.* for *complex,* and *cd.-cx.* for *compound-complex.*

EX.   *simp.*   1. The Chihuahua, named for the Mexican state of Chihuahua, is the smallest breed of dog.

_____   1. Alice Munro published her first collection of short stories in 1968; the title of that collection is *Dance of the Happy Shades.*

_____   2. After seeing the Lincoln Memorial in Washington, D. C, we stopped at the Vietnam Veterans Memorial.

_____   3. While we were on a class trip to New York City, we visited the Guggenheim Museum, which is shaped like a seashell.

_____   4. The chef said that what they tasted in the pastry crust was a secret ingredient, but he refused to reveal what it was.

_____   5. Covered with layers of straw, compost, and shredded leaves, the garden was ready for the winter.

_____   6. Toya and Derek encouraged me to join the tennis team.

_____   7. Lana never returns the books she borrows; consequently, I don't lend her my books any more.

_____   8. The young designer's collection was presented in the fall and was well received by the fashion critics.

_____   9. The scientific discovery was made in Europe, and it was widely praised there.

_____ 10. A victory over our rival football team would be a spirit booster; moreover, it is necessary if we want to make it to the state championship.

_____ 11. On live camera the news reporter described what he saw, but his account of the incident wasn't very good.

_____ 12. My grandfather, who worked for thirty years, retired in 2014.

_____ 13. When he was congratulated, the young graduate really blushed.

_____ 14. Marcia is a heavy sleeper; she sets three alarm clocks to wake up in the morning.

_____ 15. Carole introduced me to the music of Miles Davis.

MODULE 4: THE CLAUSE
MODULE REVIEW

A. Classifying Independent and Subordinate Clauses

Classify the italicized clauses in each of the sentences below. On the line before each sentence, write *indep. cl.* for *independent clause, adj. cl.* for *adjective clause, adv. cl.* for *adverb clause,* or *n. cl.* for *noun clause.*

EX. <u>*n. cl.*</u> 1. People in our department check the bulletin board weekly for *whatever messages might be posted.*

_____ 1. *Each year our family harvests and preserves cactus.*

_____ 2. We devised a system *that will promote efficiency and high productivity.*

_____ 3. *The postal carrier delivered the usual stack of junk mail.*

_____ 4. A motivating pep talk is exactly *what we need* before the next track meet.

_____ 5. *As long as we maintain this schedule*, we should meet our deadline.

_____ 6. Do you know *who is bringing the banner to the game?*

_____ 7. Tamara, *who began skiing at the age of five*, organized our high school ski club.

_____ 8. Alano closed the door to his room *so that he could read in peace.*

_____ 9. *Whenever we plan a picnic*, it rains.

_____ 10. The coach said *we could end practice early tonight.*

B. Identifying Sentence Structure

On your own paper, identify the structure of each of the sentences in the following paragraph. Write *simp.* for *simple, comp.* for *compound, cx.* for *complex,* or *cd.-cx.* for *compound-complex.*

EX. [1] Dame Agatha Christie, who was born in 1890 and died in 1976, was an English novelist and a playwright.
1. *cx.*

[1] Dame Christie began writing detective fiction during World War I, when she worked as a nurse. [2] Her two famous detective characters, Hercule Poirot and Jane Marple, appear in many of Christie's novels and short stories, but their personalities and their methods for solving murders are quite different. [3] Hercule Poirot, who first

appeared in *The Mysterious Affair at Styles*, is an odd, selfish, and foolish Belgian. [4] Christie's other famous character, Miss Jane Marple, first appeared in *Murder at the Vicarage*. [5] Miss Marple is an elderly lady; she lives in the English village of St. Mary Mead, where she enjoys gardening. [6] Dame Christie first became famous with her novel *The Murder of Roger Ackroyd*, and this book was followed by many bestsellers. [7] Many of her novels are in series form. [8] *The Mousetrap*, which is a play of Christie's, holds the record for running on stage longer than any other play. [9] Many of her works were made into successful films. [10] One of Christie's stories, which was titled "Witness for the Prosecution," was written fifty years ago, but a film based on the story continues to be popular.

C.   Working Cooperatively to Write Sentences with Varied Structure

Working with a partner, write ten sentences according to the guidelines below. Write these sentences on your own paper.

EX.   1.   a compound sentence with the conjunction *and*
       1.   *Donnie put on his pajamas, and I helped put him to bed.*

1.   a simple sentence with a compound subject
2.   a compound sentence with the conjunction *or*
3.   a complex sentence with an adverb clause that modifies a verb
4.   a complex sentence with an adverb clause that modifies an adjective
5.   a complex sentence with an adjective clause introduced by the relative pronoun *whose*
6.   a complex sentence with an adjective clause introduced by the relative pronoun *that*
7.   a complex sentence with a noun clause used as the subject of the sentence
8.   a complex sentence with a noun clause used as a direct object
9.   a complex sentence with an elliptical adverb clause
10.   a compound-complex sentence

SUBJECT-VERB AGREEMENT

5a   **A verb should agree with its subject in number.**

(1) Singular subjects take singular verbs.

EXAMPLE   The duck **swims** for the piece of bread. [The singular verb *swims* agrees with the singular subject *duck*.]

(2) Plural subjects take plural verbs.

EXAMPLE   The ducks **swim** for the piece of bread. [The plural verb *swim* agrees with the plural subject *ducks*.]

Like the one-word verb in each of the preceding examples, a verb phrase must also agree in number with its subject. The number of a verb phrase is indicated by the form of its first auxiliary (helping) verb.

EXAMPLES   My sister **is singing** a folk song. [singular subject and verb phrase]
My sisters **are singing** a folk song. [plural subject and verb phrase]
The artist **has painted** murals. [singular subject and verb phrase]
The artists **have painted** murals. [plural subject and verb phrase]

EXERCISE 1   Selecting Verbs That Agree in Number with Their Subjects

For each of the following word groups, underline the verb or verb phrase in parentheses that agrees in number with its subject.

    EX.   1.   she (*dances, dance*)

1. Carey (*works, work*)
2. they (*is driving, are driving*)
3. pineapples (*grows, grow*)
4. neighbors (*watches, watch*)
5. artist (*has woven, have woven*)
6. politicians (*debates, debate*)
7. I (*am going, is going*)
8. guests (*has been eating, have been eating*)
9. lions (*is roaring, are roaring*)
10. Raoul (*laughs, laugh*)
11. you (*has been invited, have been invited*)
12. student (*performs, perform*)
13. he (*has left, have left*)
14. storm (*is coming, are coming*)
15. mosquitoes (*buzzes, buzz*)
16. Andrew (*cooks, cook*)
17. choir (*sings, sing*)
18. rocks (*has fallen, have fallen*)
19. children (*climbs, climb*)
20. sun (*is rising, are rising*)

EXERCISE 2   Identifying Verbs That Agree in Number with Their Subjects

For each sentence below, underline the verb or verb phrase in parentheses that agrees in number with its subject.

EX.   1. That plane (*is, are*) flying low.

1. Marta (*has been reading, have been reading*) books by South American authors.

2. Can we (*swims, swim*) in the pond at the farm?

3. Johnny Appleseed, a real man, (*has become, have become*) a folk hero.

4. Her students (*studies, study*) Spanish.

5. "Do you (*knows, know*) the reason?" Tyrone asked.

6. The musicians (*has been practicing, have been practicing*) daily.

7. Because it snowed last night, the roads (*is, are*) closed this morning.

8. Anaba (*is learning, are learning*) to weave from her grandmother.

9. (*Is, Are*) the children making too much noise?

10. By watching the sky patiently, they (*was, were*) able to see a shooting star.

11. She (*was, were*) delighted by his description of wax festivals in Morocco.

12. In spring, the mountains (*is, are*) covered with wildflowers.

13. Squawking loudly, the blue jays (*scares, scare*) away smaller birds.

14. Mattie (*has won, have won*) the debate.

15. Will you see if the noodles (*is, are*) ready?

16. Mr. Jackson asked, "Why (*does, do*) you like this poem?"

17. The pianist (*is playing, are playing*) my favorite song.

18. Next summer, the Alperts (*plans, plan*) to visit Canada.

19. Here is a list of what we (*needs, need*).

20. "Look!" Mr. Wu called. "Here (*comes, come*) the dragon!"

INTERVENING PHRASES AND CLAUSES

5b **The number of the subject is not changed by a phrase or a clause following the subject.**

EXAMPLES   The **pens are** blue, green, and red.
The **pens** on the table **are** blue, green, and red. [The prepositional phrase *on the table* does not affect the number of the subject *pens*.]

The **actor has** many theater awards.
The **actor** signing autographs **has** many theater awards. [The participial phrase *signing autographs* does not affect the number of the subject *actor*.]

Delia makes wonderful knitted sweaters.
Delia, who has many talents, **makes** wonderful knitted sweaters. [The adjective clause *who has many talents* does not affect the number of the subject *Delia*.]

Prepositional phrases may begin with compound prepositions, such as *together with, in addition to, as well as,* and *along with.* These phrases do not affect the number of the verb.

EXAMPLES   **Estelle,** as well as her brothers, **is interested** in working on a farm. [singular subject and verb]
My **bags,** along with that package, **are** by the door. [plural subject and verb]

EXERCISE 3   Identifying Verbs That Agree in Number with Their Subjects

For each of the following sentences, underline the verb or verb phrase in parentheses that agrees in number with its subject.

EX.   1. The maple tree at the corner (*is turning, are turning*) beautiful colors.

1. This stack of books (*is waiting, are waiting*) to be shelved.

2. Did you know that Tena, together with her family, (*is arranging, are arranging*) the show of Navajo crafts?

3. The child, as well as her parents, (*becomes, become*) excited about summer vacation as it grows closer.

4. Ariel, along with her two brothers, (*has been preparing, have been preparing*) Seder for Passover.

5. Tany said, "The salad, as well as the enchiladas, (*looks, look*) delicious."

6. The group of senior citizens (*is visiting, are visiting*) Guam, the Philippines, and Hawaii.

7. Because the pool at school is closed, the girls on the swim team (*needs, need*) another place to practice.

8. High winds, in addition to a high tide, (*has been, have been*) predicted.

9. The first of the tour groups (*is arriving, are arriving*).

10. The report pointed out that the Comanches, as well as the Sioux, (*lives, live*) on the Great Plains.

EXERCISE 4   Proofreading a Paragraph for Correct Subject-Verb Agreement

In the paragraph below, draw a line through each verb or verb phrase that does not agree with its subject. Write the correct form of the verb or verb phrase in the space above the error. Some sentences may contain no errors in agreement.

have
EX.   [1] For Mrs. Jackson's class, the students ~~has~~ to write a report on a custom of another country.

[1] Marissa have chosen to write about Umhlanga. [2] For the girls in Swaziland, Umhlanga is a coming-of-age ceremony. [3] During this week-long event, girls travels to Lobamba, the royal city of Swaziland. [4] They gathers reeds from the riverbank. [5] The sixth day of Umhlanga are the time to prepare for a dance. [6] The girls participating in this festival wears necklaces, beaded skirts, and ankle and wrist bracelets. [7] These costumes for the Reed Dance is carefully prepared. [8] In this dance, the girls waves the reeds over their heads. [9] Onlookers, including the Queen of Swaziland, watches the girls' Reed Dance. [10] The festival, in addition to the dances, include a ceremony in which the girls use reeds to repair the fences around the Queen's residence.

MODULE 5: AGREEMENT

AGREEMENT WITH INDEFINITE PRONOUNS

5c **The following indefinite pronouns are singular:** *each, either, neither, one, everyone, everybody, no one, nobody, anyone, anybody, someone,* **and** *somebody.* **A singular indefinite pronoun takes a singular verb.**

Notice that a phrase or a clause following one of these pronouns does not affect the number of the verb.

EXAMPLES   **Everybody is** invited. [singular subject, singular verb]
Neither of them **has called** me. [singular subject, singular verb]
Anyone who has extra time **is joining** the club. [singular subject, singular verb]

5d **The following indefinite pronouns are plural:** *several, few, both,* **and** *many.* **A plural indefinite pronoun takes a plural verb.**

EXAMPLES   **Several** of my neighbors **have moved** away. [plural subject,

A **few** in the school **have participated.** [plural subject, plural verb]

5e **The following indefinite pronouns may be either singular or plural:** *some, all, any, most,* **and** *none.*

These pronouns are singular when they refer to a singular word and are plural when they refer to plural words.

EXAMPLES   **Most** of the garden **has been** planted. [*Most* refers to the singular noun *garden.*]
Most of the people **have** already seen that show. [*Most* refers to the plural noun *people.*]
All of the milk **is** sour. [*All* refers to the singular noun *milk.*]
All of the apples **have** been picked. [*All* refers to the plural noun *apples.*]
Some of the mail **is** opened. [*Some* refers to the singular noun *mail.*]
Some of the branches **are** broken. [*Some* refers to the plural noun *branches.*]

NOTE   The word *none* is singular when it means "not one" and plural when it means "not any."

EXAMPLES   **None** of the clocks **works.** [*Not one* works.]
None of the clocks **work.** [*Not any* work.]

EXERCISE 5   Identifying Subjects and Verbs That Agree in Number.

For each sentence below, underline the verb or verb phrase in parentheses that agrees in number with its subject.

EX.   1.   Most of Frank's photographs (*has been sold*, <u>*have been sold*</u>).

1. (*Is, Are*) any of those Polish dumplings left?
2. Harry said, "It looks as if many of the trails (*was, were*) closed by the landslides."
3. Several of the volunteers (*has, have*) worked all day.
4. Most of the people who have signed up for the trip (*plans, plan*) to ski.
5. Neither of the answers (*is, are*) the right one.
6. According to this chart, one of the highest mountain peaks in the world (*lie, lies*) in the Himalayas.
7. Most of these recipes (*calls, call*) for yeast.
8. All of the participants in the Braemar Highland Gathering (*wears, wear*) kilts.
9. I was glad that all of Katherine Paterson's books (*was, were*) included on the list.
10. (*Does, Do*) any of the dancers want to take a break?
11. Each of Dezba's weavings (*sells, sell*) promptly.
12. If anyone (*wants, want*) to ask questions, the speaker will stay later to answer them.
13. All of the islands in that area (*is, are*) atolls.
14. A few of the people I visit on the reservation (*remembers, remember*) a time when their lives were quite different.
15. Will both of the bands (*plays, play*) in the festival?
16. Each girl (*dances, dance*) the Sunrise Dance.
17. None of the representatives (*agrees, agree*) on a date.
18. Will everyone who (*wants, want*) a part in the play be at the audition?
19. Each of her paintings (*tells, tell*) a different legend.
20. Any winds blowing stronger than 74 miles an hour (*is, are*) considered hurricane force.

THE COMPOUND SUBJECT

A **compound subject** consists of two or more nouns or pronouns that are joined by a conjunction and have the same verb.

5f   **Subjects joined by *and* usually take a plural verb.**

Compound subjects joined by *and* that name more than one person or thing always take plural verbs.

EXAMPLES   **Marty** and **Angela have been** practicing.
             Bread, pickles, and **salad are** on the table.

Compound subjects that name only one person or one thing take a singular verb.

EXAMPLES   My favorite **actor and singer is** my friend Damien. [one person]
             Spaghetti and salad is a terrific meal. [one thing]

5g   **Singular subjects joined by *or* or *nor* take a singular verb.**

EXAMPLES   Neither **Anita** nor **Lucy works** there anymore.
             Either **Ms. Chia** or **Mr. Jackson wants** to help.

5h   **When a singular subject and a plural subject are joined by *or* or *nor*, the verb agrees with the subject nearer the verb.**

EXAMPLES   Neither my **sister** nor my **brothers are** home. [The plural subject *brothers* is nearer the verb.]
             Neither my **brothers** nor my **sister is** home. [The singular subject *sister* is nearer the verb.]

EXERCISE 6   Correcting Errors in Subject-Verb Agreement

In each of the following sentences, draw a line through any verb that does not agree in number with its subject. Write the correct form of the verb in the space above the error. Some sentences may contain no errors.

EX.   1. Either Marta or Kuzem *has* ~~have~~ the books.

1. A screwdriver and a drill is necessary for the project.

2. Neither the mangoes nor the pineapples was ripe.

3. According to our count, Susan and Harley has won the most votes.

4. Kwam's story and Tammy's poems is in the exhibition.

5. We are hoping that either Mrs. Jackson or Mr. Ortega are on the panel of judges.

6. Mandarin and Catonese is spoken in China.

7. Does either Ima or Yoshi have the information?

8. The writer and the director of the school play are Alison.

9. Joe and Kim works on a dig in Mexico during their summer vacation.

10. We read that a feast and a dance forms part of the ceremony.

11. When is Max and Mickey leaving for Canada?

12. Both the Incan and the Mayan civilizations is covered in Jolene's report.

13. Genghis Khan and Kublai Khan was Mongol leaders.

14. Two dollars and a can of food for the homeless are the price of admission.

15. Neither Lisa nor Cam run in the 50-yard dash.

16. We think that either the windows or the roof are leaking.

17. The storms and the flooding has caused severe damage.

18. Corn, beans, and avocados is grown in Mexico.

19. Both Earth and Jupiter orbits the sun.

20. Has Marla and Lee demonstrated their experiment yet?

21. Neither the principal nor the teachers enjoys long meetings after school.

22. The best coach and teacher are Ms. Yates.

23. Word processing and spread sheets is covered in the computer course.

24. Rice, noodles, spices, and seafood makes a delicious Thai main course.

25. Either the book or the magazines contains good information for your report.

EXERCISE 7 Using Verbs That Agree in Number with Compound Subjects

Write five sentences on your own paper. In each sentence, use a compound subject joined by *and, or,* or *nor.* Include one example of two singular subjects joined by *either/or* or *neither/nor* and one singular and one plural subject joined by *either/or* or *neither/nor.* Pay special attention to subject-verb agreement.

EX. 1. *My uncle and my two aunts play the piano.*

COLLECTIVE NOUNS

5i   **Collective nouns may be either singular or plural.**

A *collective noun* is singular in form, but it names a group of persons or things.

Common Collective Nouns			
army	club	group	series
assembly	committee	herd	squad
audience	crowd	jury	staff
band	faculty	majority	swarm
choir	family	number	team
class	flock	public	troop

Use a singular verb with a collective noun when you mean the group as a unit. Use a plural verb when you mean the members of the group as individuals.

EXAMPLES   The class **is** planning a picnic. [the class as a unit]
             The class **are** discussing the plans with each other. [the class members as individuals]

EXERCISE 8   Writing Sentences with Collective Nouns

From the list above, select ten collective nouns. On your own paper, write a pair of sentences using each. Each pair of sentences should show how the collective noun may be either singular or plural.

EX.   flock
   1. *a.   The flock flies over our house.*
      b.   The flock are building nests in the meadow.

REVIEW EXERCISE 1

A. Choosing Correct Verbs in Sentences

In each of the sentences below, underline the verb or verb phrase in parentheses that agrees in number with its subject.

EX. 1. Most of my friends (*likes, like*) to read.

1. The house (*seems, seem*) empty without the cat.
2. Have you noticed that the birds (*is, are*) flying south?
3. The carton of milk (*has, have*) spilled.
4. Maggie, who has traveled to many countries, (*collects, collect*) coins.
5. Strong winds, in addition to a rough surf, (*makes, make*) sailing difficult.
6. My father, as well as my two aunts, (*is, are*) coming to the show tonight.
7. Cameron and Asher (*has, have*) written a play.
8. The dogs, but not the cat, (*has, have*) been fed.
9. (*Was, Were*) all of the poems by Gwendolyn Brooks collected into one book?
10. Most of the band members (*plays, play*) more than one instrument.

B. Making Verbs Agree with Their Subjects

In each sentence below, underline any verb that does not agree in number with its subject. Then, on the line before the sentence, write the correct form of the verb. If a sentence contains no errors, write *C*.

EX. ___*is*___ 1. The audience <u>are</u> full of students and teachers.

_____ 1. Antonia and Mark has finished putting up the decorations.

_____ 2. According to this list, Angela and her brothers is coming.

_____ 3. Does anyone has a copy of Mildred D. Taylor's book?

_____ 4. The children enjoys playing with clay.

_____ 5. When the choir sing carols, it always draws a crowd.

_____ 6. As soon as Paul and Jaime arrives, we will begin.

_____ 7. Neither this chemical nor that one are what we need.

_____ 8. The unicorn, as well as the griffin, is a mythological beast.

_____ 9. Everybody who take Mrs. Chavez's class says it's really interesting.

_____ 10. The manager said that this radio, but not those, are on sale.

5j **A verb agrees with its subject, not with its predicate nominative.**

EXAMPLES A great **snack is** fresh tomatoes. [singular subject, singular verb]
Fresh **tomatoes are** a great snack. [plural subject, plural verb]

5k **When the subject follows the verb, make sure that the verb agrees with it.**

In sentences beginning with *here* or *there* and in questions, the subject follows the verb.

EXAMPLES Here **is** the **container** of berries. [singular subject, singular verb]
Here **are** the **berries**. [plural subject, plural verb]
Where **is** that **jar** of peanuts? [singular subject, singular verb]
Where **are** those **peanuts**? [plural subject, plural verb]

NOTE Contractions such as *here's, there's, how's, and what's* include the singular verb *is*. Use one of these contractions only if a singular subject follows it.

INCORRECT **There's** many **sounds** in the cafeteria. [plural subject, singular verb]
CORRECT **There's** a **lot** of noise in the cafeteria. [singular subject, singular verb]
CORRECT There **are** many **sounds** in the cafeteria. [plural subject, plural verb]

5l **An expression of an amount may be singular or plural.**

An expression of an amount is singular when the amount is thought of as a unit and is plural when the amount is thought of as many parts.

EXAMPLES **Six thousand books is** a large stock for that store. [The books are thought of as a unit.]
Six hundred books are in that store. [The books are thought of separately.]

A fraction or a percentage is singular when it refers to a singular word and is plural when it refers to a plural word.

EXAMPLES About **one third** of the crowd **is** satisfied. [The fraction refers to the singular noun *crowd*.]
About **one third** of the people in the crowd **are** satisfied. [The fraction refers to the plural noun *people*.]

Expressions of measurement (length, weight, capacity, area) are usually singular.

EXAMPLES   **Five and three-tenths inches is** the length of thread he needs.
            Three kilometers was the distance to her house.
            Four quarts equals a gallon.

NOTE   In the expression *number of,* the word *number* is singular when preceded by *the* and is plural when preceded by *a/an.*

    EXAMPLES   The **number of** people buying that product **has decreased**.
        A **number of** people **purchase** that product regularly.

5m   **The title of a creative work (such as a book, song, film, or painting) or the name of a country (even if it is plural in form) takes a singular verb.**

EXAMPLES   *The Winter Trees* **was written** by my friend Gerardo.
            The United States celebrates Memorial Day.

5n   **Many nouns that are plural in form are singular in meaning.**

(1) The following nouns always take singular verbs.

civics	genetics	news
economics	linguistics	physics
electronics	mathematics	

EXAMPLES   The **news is** on television now.
            Physics was Marta's favorite subject last year.

(2) The following nouns always take plural verbs.

binoculars	pliers	shears
eyeglasses	scissors	trousers

EXAMPLES   The **pliers are** in the kitchen drawer.
            My **trousers were torn** on a tree limb.

NOTE   Many nouns ending in *-ics,* such as *acoustics, athletics, ethics, politics, statistics,* and *tactics,* may be singular or plural.

    EXAMPLES   **Athletics is** an area in which Rhonda excels.
        Athletics are popular at my school.

If you do not know whether a noun that is plural in form is singular or plural in meaning, look in a dictionary.

5o   **The name of an organization, though plural in form, usually takes a singular verb.**

EXAMPLES   **Walker Fabrics is** a company in town.
            The **United Nations assembles** in New York City.

The names of some organizations, however, may take singular or plural verbs. When the name refers to the organization as a unit, it takes a singular verb. When the name refers to the members of the organization, it takes a plural verb.

EXAMPLES   The **San Diego Padres plays** this Saturday.
The **San Diego Padres are discussing** yesterday's game.

EXERCISE 9   Selecting Verbs That Agree in Number with Their Subjects

In each of the following sentences, underline the verb, phrase, or contraction in parentheses that agrees in number with its subject.

EX.   1.   (*Here's, Here are*) the tapes you were looking for.

1. The central character in Willa Cather's novel *O Pioneers!* (*is, are*) a pioneer woman in Nebraska.

2. The number of fish in the pond (*is, are*) unknown.

3. Physics (*attempts, attempt*) to explain matter, energy, and their interactions.

4. The Bahamas (*is, are*) a popular vacation spot.

5. We agreed that two hours (*was, were*) a long time to wait.

6. (*Where's, Where are*) the tables for the pottery display?

7. Civics (*is, are*) offered at summer school now.

8. To see the New Year's parade, a number of people (*was, were*) willing to stand in the rain.

9. A great way to spend afternoons (*is, are*) to go to the Museum of Science.

10. The children all cried, "(*Here's, Here are*) the ponies!"

11. Marilyn discovered that the mumps (*is, are*) contagious.

12. Does Raoul know that his trousers (*has, have*) been sent to the cleaners?

13. There (*is, are*) an astonishing variety of life in a rain forest.

14. The lit candles of St. Lucia's Day in Sweden (*is, are*) a beautiful sight to see.

15. To our delight, the news (*was, were*) all good.

16. *The Crusades* (*gives, give*) quite a lot of information about the Middle Ages.

17. (*Where's, Where are*) that package of tortillas I bought?

18. Takako always insists that economics (*is, are*) not as baffling as it seems.

19. The new store, Downtown Doggie Care, (*is, are*) hiring part-time help for the summer.

20. The Boston Celtics (*travels, travel*) on the same plane as we do to Chicago tomorrow.

21. (*There's, There are*) a big storm brewing at sea.

22. Fresh flowers (*adds, add*) charm to a table setting.

23. The Olympic Games (*has, have*) been held every four years.

24. Rhoda has decided that politics (*is, are*) a field in which she would like to work.

25. "Look," Bart called, "(*there's, there are*) a bear with her cubs in that meadow."

EXERCISE 10   Proofreading a Paragraph for Errors in Subject-Verb Agreement

In the paragraph below, draw a line through any verb, phrase, or contraction that does not agree in number with its subject. Write the correct form of the verb in the space above the incorrect word.

                      is

EX.   [1] Physics ~~are~~ important in the study of astronomy.

[1] I didn't know that most of the professional astronomers today has studied physics until two astronomers came to our school on Career Day. [2] The number of students waiting to talk to the astronomers were large. [3] Among the instruments the astronomers demonstrated were a small telescope. [4] Compared to a telescope, binoculars sees very little. [5] There's many planets and stars to observe with a telescope.

A.   Selecting Verbs That Agree in Number with Their Subjects

In each sentence below, underline the verb, phrase, or contraction that agrees in number with its subject.

EX.   1.   (*Where's*, <u>*Where are*</u>) the instructions for the computer?

1.   All of the planets in the solar system (*orbits*, *orbit*) the sun.

2.   *The Tombs of Atuan* (*is*, *are*) part of a trilogy by Ursula K. Le Guin.

3.   Who (*delivers*, *deliver*) the packages on Saturday?

4.   News of the earthquake (*has*, *have*) worried people who have relatives in that area.

5.   The San Francisco 49ers (*is*, *are*) in first place.

6.   For bird-watching, binoculars (*do*, *does*) help.

7.   Couscous and falafel (*was*, *were*) added to the menu.

8.   (*Here's*, *Here are*) the schedules for the Eighth Annual Polish Fest.

9.   Every member of the ballet (*practices*, *practice*) daily.

10.   *Pearls Before Swine*, the comic strip, (*entertains*, *entertain*) many readers.

11.   A number of my grandfather's roses always (*wins*, *win*) prizes.

12.   "(*How's*, *How are*) the weather in your part of the world?" he asked, as the storm howled in the background.

13.   *Nine Stories* by J. D. Salinger (*was*, *were*) discussed at our last meeting.

14.   My favorite of all of Shakespeare's plays (*is*, *are*) *The Tempest*.

15.   Three hours (*seems*, *seem*) too long for a children's party.

16.   Traditionally, when some of the Tlingit clans in Alaska (*constructs*, *construct*) a new building, they thank the spirit of the forest for the lumber.

17.   Marco's Dairy Products (*makes*, *make*) home deliveries.

18.   Four quarters (*equals*, *equal*) one dollar.

19.   Measles sometimes (*has*, *have*) serious complications.

20.   Did you know that your scissors (*needs*, *need*) sharpening?

B. Proofreading a Paragraph for Errors in Subject-Verb Agreement

In the paragraph below, draw a line through any verb, phrase, or contraction that does not agree in number with its subject. Write the correct form of the verb in the space above the error. Some sentences may contain no errors.

EX. [1] The Mayan civilization flourished in the area that today ~~are~~ *is* part of Mexico, Guatemala, and Belize.

[1] Research show that the Mayan culture was highly developed, particularly in the areas of architecture and astronomy. [2] Sites of Mayan ruins is found in the jungles of the Yucatán Peninsula. [3] Perhaps the best known site are the ruins of Chichén Itzá. [4] The remains of this ancient city draws many visitors each year. [5] The restored buildings includes a Mayan astronomical observatory. [6] A massive white stone pyramid called El Castillo, or the Temple of Kulkulcan, fills the plaza of the city. [7] Towering over the surrounding landscape, the pyramid measure eighty feet high. [8] This pyramid, like most Mayan buildings, were constructed according to strict astronomical guidelines. [9] On El Castillo, each flight of stairs have ninety-one steps. [10] The total number of steps in the stairways, in addition to the summit platform, equal 365, the number of days in a year. [11] The precision of the designs ensure that, during the spring and fall equinoxes, the setting sun lights up the eastern stairwell. [12] The sun casts a shadow that leads to the Sacred Cenote, or well. [13] Objects was cast into this well as part of the religious ceremonies. [14] Archaeologists has found all kinds of relics here. [15] Gold, silver, and jade has been taken from this well.

The word to which a pronoun refers is called its *antecedent.*

5p   **A pronoun agrees with its antecedent in gender and in number.**

(1)   **Singular pronouns refer to singular antecedents. Plural pronouns refer to plural antecedents.**

EXAMPLES   **Abraham** won **his** bicycle in a contest.
The **swimmers** took **their** gold medals with **them.**

(2)   **A few singular pronouns indicate gender (*masculine, feminine, neuter*). The singular pronouns *he, him, his*, and *himself* refer to masculine antecedents. The singular pronouns *she, her, hers*, and *herself* refer to feminine antecedents. The singular pronouns *it, its*, and *itself* refer to antecedents that are neuter (neither masculine nor feminine).**

EXAMPLES   **Roberto** put **his** coat in the closet.
Shayla has more time than **she** usually does.
Dad watered the **plant** and trimmed **its** leaves.

5q   **Singular pronouns are used to refer to the following antecedents: *anybody, anyone, each, either, everybody, everyone, neither, nobody, no one, one, somebody*, and *someone*.**

To determine the genders of these words, look in the phrases following them.

EXAMPLES   **Each** of the **boys** has offered to do **his** part.
One of the **girls** donated **her** time.

If the antecedent may be either masculine or feminine, use both masculine and feminine pronouns to refer to it.

EXAMPLES   **Everyone** who wants a ride should raise **his or her** hand.
Somebody left **his or her** books behind.

NOTE   You can often avoid the *his or her* construction by revising the sentence to use the plural forms of both the pronoun and its antecedent.

EXAMPLE   **All** of the **members** have sent **their** dues.

5r   **Use a singular pronoun to refer to two or more singular antecedents joined by *or* or *nor*.**

EXAMPLES   **Either Ralph or Peter** always walks **his** dog at the park.
Neither Mom nor Aunt Rose thinks **she** can come to the road race on Saturday.

5s   **Use a plural pronoun to refer to two or more singular antecedents joined by _and_.**

EXAMPLES   If **Monica and Leroy** want to participate, tell **them** to arrive at 7:00 P.M. sharp.

                 Cassie, Eduardo, and Liza have turned in **their** projects.

NOTE   Revise awkward constructions caused by antecedents of different genders.

        AWKWARD   Either Crystal or Ben will sing his solo.
        REVISED   Either **Crystal** will sing **her** solo, or **Ben** will sing **his.**

5t   **When a relative pronoun (_that, which_, or _who_) is the subject of an adjective clause, the verb in the clause agrees with the word to which the relative pronoun refers.**

EXAMPLES   My ballet class, **which meets** on Wednesday, is planning a recital. [_Which_ refers to the singular noun _class_.]

                 I know people **who build** boats. [_Who_ refers to the plural noun _people_.]

NOTE   When preceded by _one of [plural word]_, the relative pronoun takes a plural verb. When preceded by _the only one of [plural word]_, the relative pronoun takes a singular verb.

        EXAMPLES   _Romeo and Juliet_ is **one of the plays that are** on our reading list.

                   That novel is **the only one of the books on the list that tells** the story well.

EXERCISE 11   Proofreading for Pronouns That Agree with Their Antecedents

In each of the following sentences, fill in the blank with the pronoun (or pair of pronouns) that agrees with its antecedent.

    EX. 1. Uncle Jim planted _____*his*_____ garden yesterday.

    1. When they had finished, the workers removed _____ equipment.

    2. Somebody has volunteered _____ time to repair the fence.

    3. All of the players have had _____ checkups.

    4. Either Mari will deliver _____ speech or Ben will deliver _____.

    5. The new bicycle lost _____ shiny look after a few weeks.

    6. When Lilia and Ted arrive, tell _____ we are in the darkroom.

7. The debate team, which has a debate scheduled next Friday, will hold _____ first practice on Wednesday.

8. Anyone who wants to express _____ opinion should come to the meeting on Tuesday.

9. We told Robin she should send _____ email to the newspaper.

10. Mimi's uncle promised to give us _____ recipe for tamales.

11. The Hopi dancers will perform _____ traditional Snake Dance.

12. We know winter is coming when the maple tree in our yard starts to lose _____ leaves.

13. Neither Julie nor Amalia wants to give up _____ place.

14. Mikey, Haley, and Yori have had _____ paintings accepted for the show.

15. One of the boys has received _____ paycheck.

16. When the boat docked, we saw people on the wharf selling _____ baskets.

17. This engine has lost _____ power.

18. When the applause finally stopped, Mrs. Ortega got up to give _____ response.

19. Can he find _____ way in the dark?

20. That company makes most of _____ profits through internet sales.

21. If you want to meet two basketball players from the Indiana Pacers, you can see _____ at the restaurant tonight.

22. Each weekend, either Barry or Nick skates by on _____ in-line skates.

23. In February, the cross-country skiers will hold _____ race.

24. Each of the girls in the family sews _____ own clothes.

25. Anyone who wants to sing in the chorus may sign _____ name on the list.

EXERCISE 12   Proofreading a Paragraph for Errors in Subject-Verb and Pronoun-Antecedent Agreement

In the following paragraph, draw a line through any errors in subject-verb agreement or pronoun-antecedent agreement. Write your correction in the space above the error. Some sentences may contain no errors.

EX.   [1] One of my best and worst vacations *was* ~~were~~ the first time I went backpacking.

[1] Even now when I tries to describe it, I can't believe I ever did it. [2] The chief problem, in addition to many small complications, were that I didn't really know what I was doing. [3] Neither my friends nor I are what you would call an accomplished athlete. [4] We wanted, however, to go backpacking. [5] Paco, who reads quite a bit, say that books can teach you how to do anything. [6] We all read about how to backpack and then we set off to climb Mount Tam, which are one of the highest mountains in our area. [7] Right away, Jake and Mateo said his feet hurt, but they stopped complaining when they began to look around. [8] The views as you climb this mountain is quite spectacular. [9] As we was admiring the view, however, Paco said, "It looks like there are clouds forming in the west." [10] The storm hit just as we was setting up our camp for the night. [11] We tried to pitch our tent quickly, but we had lost his stakes, and so it was useless. [12] Do you has any idea how hard it is to find a dry shelter during a wild storm? [13] We found a cave, but in our rush, we left our packs of food lying out on the ground. [14] I only hope that the two bears who found the food enjoyed its dinner. [15] As we huddled, cold and hungry in our cave, Paco said, "I'll have to read a few more books before we try this again."

MODULE REVIEW

A. Proofreading Sentences for Subject-Verb and Pronoun-Antecedent Agreement

In each of the sentences below, draw a line through any errors in subject-verb agreement and pronoun-antecedent agreement. Then, on the line before the sentence, write your correction. If a sentence contains no errors, write *C*.

EX. _____*have*_____   1. Most of the people that we've invited ~~has~~ accepted.

_____   1. Here's the ingredients you needed for the chile.

_____   2. Gillian, but not her brothers, works in her father's shop.

_____   3. Neither Steve nor Jorge has memorized their lines.

_____   4. Ten dollars are too much to pay for that print.

_____   5. Because of the storms, that trail have been closed.

_____   6. Every table has their assigned display items.

_____   7. The news are good about funds for the basketball court.

_____   8. There's a new set of books that arrived this morning.

_____   9. Toby noticed that your shears is in the box.

_____   10. Mathematics are a subject that Jamillah understands easily.

_____   11. Is these roads through the jungle paved?

_____   12. His ten minutes are up.

_____   13. Unfortunately, measles are going around the school.

_____   14. Do you think Cora have a good chance to win the election?

_____   15. Each of my sisters has their day planned.

_____   16. The tent and the sleeping bags is packed.

_____   17. My cats, as well as my dog, needs to go for a walk every day.

_____   18. That bag of clothes are for the rummage sale

_____   19. Some of the dishes was chipped.

_____   20. *The Canterbury Tales* make me laugh aloud at times.

B. Proofreading a Paragraph for Errors in Subject-Verb and Pronoun-Antecedent Agreement

In the paragraph below, draw a line through any errors in subject-verb agreement or pronoun-antecedent agreement. Write the corrections on your own paper. Some sentences may contain no errors.

EX.　[1] One of the most unusual athletic competitions are the Frog Jumping Contest.
　　　1. *is*

[1] The event take place each year in the foothills of California. [2] This is the area where gold were discovered in 1849, causing the California Gold Rush. [3] Mark Twain, in addition to many other writers, have written about this exciting time in California's history. [4] Twain wrote a story called "The Celebrated Jumping Frog of Calaveras County." [5] Jim Smiley and his frog is the main characters in this story. [6] Smiley claim his frog can outjump any other frog. [7] The town of Angel's Camp began sponsoring frog-jumping contests after the story were published. [8] Each year now, as many as three thousand frogs participates in this competition. [9] Tourists and residents makes a huge, enthusiastic audience. [10] The frog that jumps the farthest three times in a row win the Grand Finals.

C. Writing a Sales Report

As the assistant manager of the Chop Wok Cafe, you have to write a weekly sales report. On your own paper, use the information below to write a report that has five sentences. Be sure your subjects and verbs agree in number.

EX. *Shrimp with noodles and cashew chicken were the most popular items.*

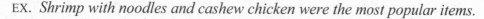

MODULE 6: CORRECT PRONOUN USAGE

CASE OF PRONOUNS

Case is the form that a noun or a pronoun takes to indicate its use in a sentence. In English, there are three cases: *nominative, objective*, and *possessive*.

The form of the noun is the same for both the nominative case and the objective case. For example, a noun used as a subject (nominative case) will have the same form if used as an object (objective case).

NOMINATIVE CASE   The **student** gave her speech. [subject]

OBJECTIVE CASE   Give the **student** your attention. [indirect object]

A noun changes its form for the possessive case, usually by adding an apostrophe and an s to most singular nouns and only the apostrophe to most plural nouns.

POSSESSIVE CASE   I enjoyed the **student's** speech. [singular]
I enjoyed the **students'** speeches. [plural]

PERSONAL PRONOUNS		
Singular		
Nominative Case	**Objective Case**	**Possessive Case**
I	me	my, mine
you	you	your, yours
he, she, it	him, her, it	his, her, hers, its
Plural		
Nominative Case	**Objective Case**	**Possessive Case**
we	us	our, ours
you	you	your, yours
they	them	their, theirs

Notice in the chart that *you* and *it* have the same form in the nominative and the objective case. All other personal pronouns have different forms for each case. Notice also that only third person singular pronouns indicate gender.

NOTE   Some teachers prefer to call possessive pronouns, such as *my*, adjectives. Follow your teacher's directions in labeling possessive forms.

EXERCISE 1 Classifying Personal Pronouns

On the line before each sentence below, identify the case of the italicized pronoun by writing *nom.* for *nominative, obj.* for *objective,* or *poss.* for *possessive.*

EX. ___poss.___ 1. We admired *her* photographs.

_____ 1. Have you finished *your* report on Guatemala?

_____ 2. *We* planted a community garden this year.

_____ 3. These seats are *theirs.*

_____ 4. When I saw *him* yesterday, Jasper said he would be gone for a week.

_____ 5. *They* pointed the telescope at Mars.

_____ 6. "Is this *his* project?" the judges asked.

_____ 7. Grandma Moses began painting when *she* was in her seventies.

_____ 8. In Japan, farmers plant trees in *their* rice fields for good luck.

_____ 9. The guard told *us* where to find the room with the Egyptian statues.

_____ 10. Because Wallace is such a good speaker, we have elected *him* our representative.

_____ 11. *Our* ideas for what to do with the vacant lot are on the list of possibilities.

_____ 12. *My* recipe for gazpacho is delicious.

_____ 13. When Asa plays his guitar, *he* always draws a crowd.

_____ 14. The Seminole people have traditionally celebrated *their* new corn crop with the Green Corn Dance.

_____ 15. According to this report, *they* have changed their minds again.

_____ 16. *I* think it's going to rain.

_____ 17. I think that this battery has lost *its* power.

_____ 18. Today *we* are going to hear their speeches.

_____ 19. "The best notes to read are *hers,*" Mrs. Jackson said.

_____ 20. The swimming power of a shark comes from *its* tail.

MODULE 6: CORRECT PRONOUN USAGE
NOMINATIVE CASE PRONOUNS

6a   **The subject of a verb is in the nominative case.**

EXAMPLES   **I** organize the file cabinets. [*I* is the subject of *organize*.]

Darnell and she raked leaves. [*Darnell and she* is the compound subject of *raked*.]

They saw that **we** worked hard on the project. [*They* is the subject of *saw*, and *we* is the subject of *worked*.]

A subject may be a compound, with a pronoun appearing in combination with a noun or another pronoun. To help you choose the correct pronoun form in a compound subject, try each form as the simple subject of the verb.

EXAMPLE   (*She, Her*) and (*I, me*) learned to square dance.

Her and *me* learned to square dance. [incorrect use of objective case]

She and *I* learned to square dance. [correct use of nominative case]

ANSWER   **She** and **I** learned to square dance.

6b   **A predicate nominative is in the nominative case.**

A *predicate nominative* is a noun or pronoun that follows a linking verb and explains or identifies the subject of the sentence. A pronoun used as a predicate nominative always follows a form of the verb *be* or a verb phrase ending in *be* or *been*.

EXAMPLES   The coach of the team is **she.** [*She* follows the linking verb *is* and identifies the subject *coach*.]

The fastest worker has been **he.** [*He* follows the linking verb *has been* and identifies the subject *worker*.]

The third place winners were **he** and **I.** [*He* and *I* follow the linking verb *were* and identify the subject *winners*.]

NOTE   In casual conversation, expressions such as *It's me* and *That's her* are acceptable. Avoid them in more formal speaking situations, such as job interviews. In your written work, do not use them unless you are creating casual conversation in dialogue.

EXERCISE 2   Using Personal Pronouns as Subjects and Predicate Nominatives

For each of the following sentences, underline the correct personal pronoun in parentheses.

EX.   1.   The best writers are (<u>*they*</u>, *them*).

1. (*She, Her*) and I are painting the signs.

2. Have (*they, them*) finished their float for the New Year's parade?

3. Will you see if it is (*they, them*) at the door?

4. Her grandfather and (*she, her*) both play the violin.

5. It was (*he, him*) who recommended that we stop in the Rockies on our way to California.

6. Of course, you and (*he, him*) are invited to the party.

7. If you climb the ladder, (*her, she*) and I will hold it.

8. Like Chim, (*he, him*) was born in Vietnam.

9. Even though I'd lost the map, (*they, them*) and I found our way back through Veracruz to our hotel.

10. Is it (*she, her*) who is going to tell stories about Kwanzaa for the holiday program?

EXERCISE 3   Proofreading for the Correct Use of Pronouns in the Nominative Case

In the paragraph below, draw a line through each incorrect pronoun form. Write the correct pronoun in the space above the word. Some sentences are correct.

EX.   [1] When Sam and ~~me~~ *I* go to visit his grandmother, she often tells us about the books she is illustrating.

[1] It was her who drew all the pictures for a popular series of books about

American Indian peoples. [2] Right now her project is a book about the Iroquois. [3]

The author and her work closely together. [4] She said that she and him talk on the

phone several times a day. [5] When Sam and me were at her house last week, we

learned that they are working on a module about the Midwinter Ceremony of the

Iroquois. [6] We saw the drawings that her was making of the masks worn in this ceremony. [7] Sam's grandmother said that when the Iroquois wear these masks, them become "curing spirits." [8] She showed Sam and me some masks that the author and her had borrowed to study. [9] Him and I each had a favorite. [10] Sam tried one on, but I didn't.

MODULE 6: CORRECT PRONOUN USAGE

OBJECTIVE CASE PRONOUNS

6c **A direct object and an indirect object are in the objective case.**

A *direct object* is a noun or pronoun that receives the action of the verb or shows the result of the action.

EXAMPLES   The letter made **her** happy. [*Her* tells whom the letter made happy.]
Lacey reported **it** to the police. [*It* tells what Lacey reported.]

An *indirect object* is a noun or pronoun that tells *to whom* or *for whom* or *to what* or *for what* the action of the verb is done.

EXAMPLES   Mr. Jardim told **them** a wonderful story. [*Them* tells *to whom* Mr. Jardim told a wonderful story.]
Greta brought **him** a map to the stadium. [*Him* tells *for whom* Greta brought a map.]

6d **An object of a preposition is in the objective case.**

A noun or pronoun used as an *object of a preposition* comes at the end of a phrase that begins with a preposition.

EXAMPLES   with **her**   next to **me**   beside **you** and **me**

To choose the correct pronoun in a compound direct object, compound indirect object, or compound object of a preposition, try each form of the pronoun separately in a sentence.

EXAMPLE   Julio surprised him and I.
Julio surprised him. [correct]
Julio surprised I. [incorrect]
ANSWER   Julio surprised **him** and **me.**

EXAMPLE   The man gave directions to them and we.
The man gave directions to them. [correct]
The man gave directions to we. [incorrect]
ANSWER   The man gave directions to **them** and **us.**

EXERCISE 4   Selecting Correct Forms of Objective Case Pronouns

For each sentence below, underline the correct form of the personal pronoun in parentheses.

EX.   1.   Kiwa told her and (*I*, *me*) that the book is good.

1.   When it began to rain, Max lent them and (*we*, *us*) umbrellas for the walk home.

2.   Matsuo can sit with (*her*, *she*) if she needs a translator.

3.   The owl surprised Harry and (*he*, *him*) as it swooped down from the tree.

4.   According to the program, they will present the award to (*she*, *her*) after the band has played.

5.   Lani brought pineapples to (*they*, *them*) when she came back from Hawaii.

6.   Ms. Goldstein has encouraged him and (*me*, *I*) to see that play.

7.   Regina said the fireworks frightened the cat and (*she*, *her*).

8.   After Anwar and (*me*, *I*), you are scheduled to perform.

9.   After George had unpacked the dishes, he carefully arranged (*they*, *them*) on the exhibit table.

10.   The police praised Tamara and (*he*, *him*) for their quick thinking.

11.   Will you lend (*we*, *us*) your dishes for the tea ceremony?

12.   He told (*we*, *us*) the story of Sojourner Truth.

13.   "Have you given the package to (*he*, *him*)?" Tome asked.

14.   As they climbed the steps of the old house, Tim fell behind Lily and (*she*, *her*).

15.   In his cooking lesson today, Ken showed (*we*, *us*) how to fix bean curd.

16.   Has anyone else signed up for the backpacking trip with you and (*I*, *me*)?

17.   That letter should be addressed to (*she*, *her*) as well.

18.   Because Ramona worked so hard getting ready for the festival, Mrs. Gutierrez gave (*she*, *her*) extra tickets.

19.   I gave (*they*, *them*) the guidebooks for the pyramids.

20.   Will you tell Franklin that he can ride to the museum with (*I*, *me*)?

REVIEW EXERCISE

A.   Identifying Correct Pronoun Forms

In each of the sentences below, underline the correct pronoun in parentheses. On the line before each sentence, identify the pronoun's use in the sentence. Write s. for *subject, p.n.* for *predicate nominative, d.o.* for *direct object, i.o.* for *indirect object,* or *o.p.* for *object of a preposition.*

EX. ____*s.*____   1.   Mrs. Chen and (*I, me*) often walk home together.

_____   1.   Can you give (*we, us*) directions?

_____   2.   He and (*I, me*) are going to make guacamole for the booth at the fair.

_____   3.   Before the sun had risen, Sanchez had wakened the rest of (*we, us*) with the wonderful smells of the breakfast he was cooking.

_____   4.   It was (*I, me*) who dropped the keys in the snow.

_____   5.   When a family from Chile moved next door, my mother and (*I, me*) decided to call them.

_____   6.   Thanks to (*him, he*) we have plenty of flowers for decorations.

_____   7.   The children gave (*she, her*) a lantern they had made for the Lantern Festival.

_____   8.   Mrs. Roosevelt entertained (*we, us*) with her stories about traveling in foreign countries.

_____   9.   When she left, the villagers thanked (*she, her*) for her help with gifts of fruit and seashells.

_____   10.   Didn't you know it was (*I, me*) in that costume?

B.   Proofreading for Correct Pronouns

In the following paragraph, draw a line through each pronoun that is used incorrectly. Write the correct form in the space above it. Not all sentences contain errors.

              We

EX.   [1] ~~Us~~ wrote a paper about wolves.

    [1] Clay and me wrote to different organizations that are trying to protect wolves

today. [2] They sent we quite a lot of information about wolves. [3] I read that Native

Americans respect wolves and have learned about survival from them. [4] The Lakota

Sioux call they "the animal who looks like a dog but is a powerful spirit." [5] Other people, however, feared wolves and tried to destroy they. [6] Today, wolves are endangered in the United States (except in Alaska and Minnesota), and in many other parts of the world where them once lived. [7] It was me who got the idea to go see some wolves at a nearby wildlife center. [8] Clay thought it was a great idea, although he admitted that he was nervous about being close to a wolf. [9] The director, however, went right into a yard full of they. [10] Clay and I have found that wolves can be both dangerous and shy.

C.   Working Cooperatively to Write a Report

You and a partner are co-chairpersons for the See the World Fair that is being held in your school. Work together to write a report of at least fifteen sentences for your class sponsor, explaining your committee's ideas for running the fair. For prewriting, fill in ideas for the categories below. In your report, include one example of each of the three cases of pronouns you have just studied. Underline and label each pronoun (*nom.* for *nominative, obj.* for *objective*, or *poss.* for *possessive.*) Write your report on your own paper.

EX. Games *nom.* *We will need several different kinds of *obj.* them for young children.*

Type of Booth

Decorations for Booth

Shifts for Working at Booth

People for Shifts

Costumes for Workers

Food

Crafts

MODULE 6: CORRECT PRONOUN USAGE
POSSESSIVE CASE PRONOUNS

6e **The possessive pronouns *mine, yours, his, hers, its, ours*, and *theirs* are used in the same ways that the pronouns in the nominative and the objective cases are used.**

SUBJECT	Your book and **mine** are getting worn.
PREDICATE NOMINATIVE	That bicycle is **his.**
DIRECT OBJECT	I cleaned **theirs** first.
INDIRECT OBJECT	Please give **ours** a try.
OBJECT OF PREPOSITION	Did I put my coat under **yours?**

6f **The possessive pronouns *my, your, his, her, its, our*, and *their* are used as adjectives before nouns.**

EXAMPLES **My** hat is ripped.
His water is boiling.
Did you know **our** address changed?

6g **A noun or a pronoun preceding a gerund is in the possessive case.**

A *gerund* is a verb form that ends in *–ing* and functions as a noun. Since a gerund acts as a noun, the noun or pronoun that comes before it must be in the possessive case in order to modify the gerund.

EXAMPLES **Their** careful planning was helpful. [*Their* modifies the gerund *planning*. Whose planning? Their planning.]
I was concerned about **his** jogging on that busy street. [*His* modifies the gerund *jogging*. Whose jogging? His jogging.]

Do not confuse a gerund with a present participle, which is also a verb form that ends in *–ing*. A gerund acts as a noun; a present participle serves as an adjective. A noun or pronoun that is modified by a present participle should not be in the possessive case.

EXAMPLE We watched **people** dancing around the room. [*People* is modified by the participial phrase *dancing around the room*.]

The form of a noun or pronoun before an *–ing* word often depends on the meaning you want to express. If you want to emphasize the *–ing* word, use the possessive form. If you want to emphasize the noun or pronoun preceding the *–ing* word, avoid the possessive form.

EXAMPLES The **Cooking Club's** planning a community dinner received praise. [The emphasis is on the gerund *planning*. *Cooking Club's* modifies *planning*.]
The **Cooking Club** planning a community dinner received praise. [The emphasis is on *Cooking Club*. The participle *planning* modifies *Cooking Club*.]

EXERCISE 5   Using Possessive Nouns and Pronouns

In each of the sentences below, underline the correct noun or pronoun in parentheses. Be prepared to explain why you chose the word you did.

EX.   1.   The entire group listened to (<u>his</u>, him) teachings.

1. After the applause stopped, she began (her, hers) reading.

2. (Kwan, Kwan's) cooking always wins praise.

3. "His order and (your, yours) are ready," the clerk said.

4. (His, Him) fast driving on the mountain roads made us a little nervous.

5. When it was time for the reports, Ming was the first to read us (her, hers).

6. To watch my (grandfather, grandfather's) dancing the tango is a treat.

7. (Ours, Our) digging resulted in a fine snow cave.

8. The second time we tried (our, ours) experiment, it worked perfectly.

9. Frank said he was kept awake all night by the (frogs, frogs') croaking.

10. (Their, Them) dancing was the highlight of the program.

11. Someone finally mentioned that (their, them) giggling disturbed the audience.

12. We watched the (lights, lights') twinkling from the dragon boats.

13. Gloomily, we watched the (bears, bears') escaping with our fish.

14. Did you hear the (bells, bells') ringing at midnight?

15. After looking at all the presents, Maria decided to open (their, theirs) first.

16. I added my donation to (her, hers).

17. I tried to count the number of (lilies, lilies') floating in the pool.

18. Joel discovered that the books he thought were his were actually (my, mine).

19. "(His, Him) giving so much time to this project made all the difference," the speaker said, as he gave the flowers to Mr. Valliere.

20. We admired (Emily, Emily's) constant practicing.

SPECIAL PRONOUN PROBLEMS

6h **Pronouns used as appositives should be in the same case as the word they refer to.**

An *appositive* is a noun or pronoun used with another noun or pronoun to identify or explain it.

EXAMPLES The captains, **he** and **she**, should introduce the players. [The pronouns are in the nominative case because they are in apposition with the subject *captains*.]
The award was given to the entire group, **him, her,** and **me.** [The pronouns are in the objective case because they are in apposition with the object of the preposition *group*.]

6i **A pronoun following *than* or *as* in an elliptical construction is in the same case as it would be if the construction were completed.**

An *elliptical construction* is a clause from which words have been omitted.

ELLIPTICAL Chad was much more careful on the ice **than she.**
COMPLETED Chad was much more careful on the ice **than she was.**

ELLIPTICAL The annoying noise bothered Anastasia as much **as him.**
COMPLETED The annoying noise bothered Anastasia as much **as it bothered him.**

The pronoun form in an elliptical construction determines the meaning of the elliptical phrase or clause. Be sure to use the pronoun form that expresses the meaning you intend. Notice how the meaning of each of the following sentences depends on the pronoun form in the elliptical construction.

EXAMPLES I have been Carter's neighbor longer **than he.** [I have been Carter's neighbor longer *than he has been Carter's neighbor.*]
I have been Carter's neighbor longer **than his.** [I have been Carter's neighbor longer *than I have been his neighbor.*]

6j **A pronoun ending in *–self* or *–selves* should not be used in place of a simple personal pronoun.**

NONSTANDARD Wally and **myself** decorated the gym.
STANDARD Wally and **I** decorated the gym.

EXERCISE 6   Selecting the Correct Pronouns

For each of the following sentences, underline the correct pronoun in parentheses.

EX.   1.   She gave the flowers to Winston and (*me, myself*).

1. Rachel has studied French longer than (*she, her*).

2. Please give a medal to each of the finalists, Hena and (*he, him*).

3. The two who have been to Kenya, she and (*I, me*), prepared some of the foods we'd eaten there.

4. The captain let the crew, (*he, him*) and me, take a break.

5. The Sherpa guides, both (*she, her*) and he, carried the heavy packs.

6. "Have you been waiting as long as (*I, me*)?" the woman asked worriedly.

7. When we went bird-watching with Derek, no one saw as many birds as (*he, him*).

8. Vanessa gave Troy and (*me, myself*) some photos she'd taken at the ocean.

9. We invited all the neighborhood children, (*they, them*) and their families, to the fair.

10. The best swimmers of the group, you and (*he, him*), should try out for the team.

11. Jeremy and (*I, myself*) plan to explore the caves.

12. Liam was more cautious than (*her, she*) about swimming out too far.

13. The reporter wants to talk to people who saw the accident, (*they, them*) and you.

14. The scientists will demonstrate their experiment for those who are interested, you and (*I, me*).

15. The Robinsons have been living in that neighborhood as long as (*they, them*).

16. Aunt Hannah told us how they, (*her, she*) and her cousins, used to go for sleigh rides in Poland.

17. Those two people, she and (*he, him*), are the authors of the book we've been reading.

18. There have been several articles in the school newspaper about Jamal and (*me, myself*).

19. It takes me twice as long as (*her, she*) to read Chinese.

20. My grandmother likes going to concerts as much as (*I, me*).

21. George has been to Denmark as many times as (*we, us*).

22. The coach gave both teams, them and (*we, us*), the day off.

23. They set off to climb the same mountain, but they went much farther than (*we, us*).

24. All of the Guatemalan villagers, (*they, them*) and their prayer leader, participated in the ceremony to protect their crops.

25. Can you lend your notes from history class to Samantha and (*him, himself*)?

MODULE 6: CORRECT PRONOUN USAGE

WHO *AND* WHOM

Like most personal pronouns, the pronoun *who* (*whoever*) has three case forms.

Nominative	Objective	Possessive
who whoever	whom whomever	whose whosever

6k These pronouns are called *interrogative pronouns* when they are used to form a question. When they are used to introduce subordinate clauses, they are called *relative pronouns*.

(1) The form an interrogative pronoun takes depends on its use in a question.

Who is used as a subject or as a predicate nominative. *Whom* is used as an object of a verb or as an object of a preposition.

NOMINATIVE   **Who** wants to see the show? [*Who* is the subject of the verb *wants*.]

OBJECTIVE   With **whom** did you jog? [*Whom* is the object of the preposition *with*.]

NOTE   In spoken English, the use of *whom* is gradually disappearing. Nowadays it is acceptable to begin a spoken question with *who* regardless of whether the nominative or the objective form is grammatically correct. In writing, though, it is still important to distinguish between *who* and *whom*.

(2) The form a relative pronoun takes depends on its use in a subordinate clause.

To choose between *who* or *whom* in a subordinate clause, follow these steps.
Step 1:   Find the subordinate clause.
Step 2:   Decide how the relative pronoun is used in the clause—*subject, predicate nominative, direct object, indirect object*, or *object of a preposition*.
Step 3:   Determine the case for this use of the relative pronoun.
Step 4:   Select the correct case form of the relative pronoun.

EXAMPLE   She is the one (*who, whom*) I met yesterday.
Step 1:   The subordinate clause is (*who, whom*) *I met yesterday.*
Step 2:   In this clause, the pronoun is the direct object of the verb *met.*
Step 3:   As a direct object, the pronoun should be in the objective case.
Step 4:   The objective form is *whom.*
ANSWER   She is the one **whom** I met yesterday.

EXERCISE 7   Using *Who* and *Whom* Correctly

In the sentences below, underline the correct form of the pronoun in parentheses.

EX.   1. (*Who*, *Whom*) did you wish to see?

1. Julian Bond was a politician (*who*, *whom*) I admire.
2. We will give a prize to (*whoever*, *whomever*) enters the contest.
3. (*Who*, *Whom*) is in charge of selling tickets?
4. Do you know (*who*, *whom*) the prime minister of Canada is?
5. To (*who*, *whom*) shall we send this letter?
6. William Jay Smith, (*who*, *whom*) was a well-known poet, also wrote about how sounds influenced his writing.
7. After I visited the Sierra Nevada, I began to read about John Muir, (*who*, *whom*) was an early conservationist.
8. We wrote to Mrs. Ramírez, the potter (*who*, *whom*) we met last summer, asking her to visit our school.
9. Can you guess (*who*, *whom*) is going to win the election?
10. Is it Ms. Jefferson (*who*, *whom*) is planning to travel through Africa?
11. The International Club mailed invitations to (*whoever*, *whomever*) had signed up for a language class.
12. I'd really like to know (*who*, *whom*) the artists are.
13. Suni is the only one (*who*, *whom*) got a perfect score on the test.
14. The basketball player (*who*, *whom*) I wrote to sent an autographed photo to sell at our fund-raiser.
15. Flo is going on vacation with the Yamotos, (*who*, *whom*) she has known for several years.
16. The governor said, "I need someone on (*who*, *whom*) I can depend absolutely."
17. The hikers greeted (*whoever*, *whomever*) they passed on the trail.
18. Everyone asked, "(*Who*, *Whom*) is he?"
19. Josie can't decide (*who*, *whom*) she will chose for a partner.
20. "Pardon me," the newcomer said. "To (*who*, *whom*) do I pay my entrance fee?"

MODULE 6: CORRECT PRONOUN USAGE
MODULE REVIEW

A.   Proofreading Sentences for Correct Pronoun Forms

In each of the sentences below, draw a line through any incorrect pronoun forms. On the line before the sentence, write the correct form of the pronoun. If the sentence contains no errors, write *C*.

EX. ____*her*____ 1.   Will you play baseball with Jesse and ~~she~~?

_____   1.   Whom made this painting of the sunset?

_____   2.   Leo and myself hope to go to Alaska.

_____   3.   Carla went on more rides than him at the carnival.

_____   4.   Before the game started, the captains, him and I, shook hands.

_____   5.   The winner of the writing contest is she.

_____   6.   White Feather told Hy and I stories about his ancestors.

_____   7.   Her and Lizzie are going to light the menorah.

_____   8.   When we got to the top, we saw that Luna and him were there.

_____   9.   Tina, who I saw yesterday, said the rehearsal is at noon.

_____ 10.   I wish I practiced as much as him.

_____ 11.   Jason and myself are going to audition for parts in the play.

_____ 12.   The two who designed the experiment, her and I, will be testing it tomorrow.

_____ 13.   Gloria and them are going to the swim meet.

_____ 14.   It might have been him who left this message.

_____ 15.   We kept the party a secret so that it would surprise her and he.

B.   Proofreading a Paragraph for Correct Pronoun Forms

In the following paragraph, draw a line through each incorrect pronoun form. In the space above it, write the correct form of the pronoun. Not all sentences contain errors.

EX.   [1] Everyone said it was the chance of a lifetime when Tess and $\overset{I}{\text{~~me~~}}$ were invited to visit Greenland.

[1] Her uncle is a mountaineer and a man who I admire a lot. [2] It was quite

amazing that he would include Tess and myself in one of his adventures. [3] Tess's mother, who is a photographer, wanted to go with he and his expedition on their first

trip to Greenland. [4] She persuaded him to include Tess and I. [5] Us three, Tess, her

mother and I, worked hard to get in shape for this trip inside the Arctic Circle. [6] I

didn't know anyone whom had ever gone to Greenland, but I found some books to

read about it. [7] First, we had to fly to Iceland to get a flight to Greenland. [8] While

Tess's uncle made final preparations for the climb, Tess, her mother, and me explored

the town of Ilulissat. [9] Tess and I met an Inuit girl who was not much older than us.

[10] Tess's mom took several photographs of Tess and I with our new friend.

C.   Writing About Community Service

Your local newspaper wants to interview you, the chairperson of last weekend's clean-up
project at your neighborhood park. On the lines below, write ten sentences to use as notes
during your interview. Include details about people who helped you and refreshments or
tools and supplies they brought. Use pronouns from all three cases. Also be sure to use
forms of *who/whom* and pronoun appositives. Underline all the pronouns you use.

EX.   *My best friends, Paulo and Shannon, <u>who</u> brought rakes and trash bags for <u>us</u>
to use, worked hard all day long.*

_____

_____

_____

_____

_____

_____

_____

_____

_____

_____

_____

MODULE 7: CLEAR REFERENCE
AMBIGUOUS REFERENCE

A pronoun has no definite meaning in itself. Its meaning is clear only when the reader knows what word it stands for. The word that a pronoun stands for is called the *antecedent* of the pronoun.

7a   A pronoun should always refer clearly to its antecedent.

In the following examples, arrows point from the pronouns to their antecedents.

EXAMPLES   After **Bonny** sang the aria, the audience applauded **her.**

Would a window box help **us** brighten up **our** kitchen?

Tying the **boat** to the mooring, Tiwa said, "**It** should be safe here."

(1) Avoid an *ambiguous reference*, which occurs when a pronoun refers to either of two antecedents.

AMBIGUOUS   Our friends asked the Wongs if they could show them the map. [The antecedents of *they* and *them* are unclear.]

CLEAR   Our **friends** asked if the Wongs could show **them** the map.

CLEAR   Our **friends** asked if **they** could show the map to the Wongs.

AMBIGUOUS   The teacher discussed with Eloise the exercise she had just written on the whiteboard. [The antecedent of *she* is unclear.]

CLEAR   After the **teacher** had written the exercise on the whiteboard, **she** discussed it with Eloise.

CLEAR   After **Eloise** had written the exercise on the whiteboard, the teacher discussed it with **her.**

(2) Avoid a *general reference*, which occurs when a pronoun refers to a general idea rather than to a specific noun.

The pronouns commonly used in making general references are *it, this, that, which,* and *such.*

GENERAL   Raoul could dance, sing, and play the violin. The judges awarded him first prize in the talent show for **this.** [*This* has no specific antecedent.]

CLEAR   Raoul could dance, sing, and play the violin. The judges awarded him first prize in the talent show for **his many abilities.**

CLEAR   **Because Raoul could dance, sing, and play the violin,** the judges awarded him first prize in the talent show.

GENERAL   The team has won every game this season, and we think **it's** terrific. [*It's* has no specific antecedent.]

CLEAR   We think **it's** terrific **that the team has won every game this season.**

EXERCISE 1 Revising Sentences to Correct Ambiguous and General References

On your own paper, rewrite each of the sentences below, correcting the ambiguous or general pronoun references.

EX. 1. Chet was joking with Angelo when he should have been fixing the car.
1. *Instead of joking with Angelo, Chet should have been fixing the car.*

1. Jeremy congratulated the chef for his wonderful cooking, which made him quite happy.

2. Mindy waved to Roberta as she came out of the store.

3. We saw jugglers, acrobats, and clowns at the circus, which was very entertaining.

4. Many people disapproved of the candidate's political ideas, and it cost him the election.

5. Albert told Oscar that he'd brought the wrong book.

6. When our lawyer brought the expert to lunch, we asked him to show us the report.

7. Dolores was going to pick up the baby, but then she fell asleep.

8. I sent in three box tops and the answer to the riddle. That could win the contest.

9. The lights went out and we heard a strange sound, which made us jump.

10. Hector and Philip get along well because of his interest in sports.

11. The manager was a smooth talker and a stylish dresser, which everybody knew.

12. Our team raced against the Midvale All-Stars the year they set the league record.

13. We study hard and practice a lot, which is why we're the best.

14. Georgianna heard the news during the bumpy train ride, and it made her feel sick.

15. Choy sent a text message to Ling even though he didn't know him.

7b Avoid a *weak reference*, which occurs when a pronoun refers to an antecedent that has not been expressed.

WEAK   We went to the automobile show yesterday, and Dad couldn't decide which of them he liked the best. [The antecedent of *them* is not expressed.]

CLEAR   We went to the automobile show yesterday, and Dad couldn't decide which of the **cars** he liked the best.

WEAK   Ruben was in training to run that marathon, but this year it was canceled.

CLEAR   Ruben was in training to run that marathon, but this year the **race** was canceled.

7c In formal writing, avoid the indefinite use of the pronouns *it, they,* and *you.*

An indefinite reference occurs when a pronoun refers to no particular person or thing. Such a pronoun is unnecessary to the meaning of the sentence.

INDEFINITE   In the message it said he should report immediately. [*It* has no clear antecedent in the sentence.]

CLEAR   The message said he should report immediately.

INDEFINITE   In most surveys, they use a balanced sample. [*They* is not necessary to the meaning of the sentence.]

CLEAR   Most surveys use a balanced sample.

INDEFINITE   You aren't shown any of the credits until the end in some modern films. [*You* has no clear antecedent in the sentence.]

CLEAR   Some modern films don't show any credits until the end.

NOTE   The indefinite use of *it* in familiar expressions such as *it is morning, it is raining, it seems,* and *it is warm* is acceptable.

EXERCISE 2   Revising Sentences to Correct Weak and Indefinite References

On your own paper, rewrite each of the following sentences, correcting the weak or indefinite pronoun reference.

    EX.   1. High in those mountains, you will discover the air is quite thin.

              1. *High in those mountains, the air is quite thin.*

1. Sheila is always excited about something, and one of them in particular is basketball.

2. It was a cloudy day, and we thought it might rain if they got any darker.

3. On the radio they said the war was over.

4. On that Caribbean island, you have nothing short of a tropical paradise.

5. Rinaldo was a fine tailor and made sure they were always mended on time.

6. On the back of the carton, it said, "Do not bend."

7. In my garden, they always bloom.

8. We rode in the car for six hours, and it made us tired.

9. Meet me at the train station, and we'll take it home together.

10. In some countries, they already have government-run health-care plans.

11. Frederico was known as the finest swordsman in the land, but he never drew it in anger.

12. The story said that on some planets they had strange creatures.

13. The telephone operator told me to stay on the line, and she would put it through for me.

14. In *The New York Times*, they reported on the peace talks.

15. We often look at the sky at night, but only astronomers using telescopes can always see them.

16. It was mentioned in the newsletter that Ryan had been promoted.

17. They never caught Jesse James.

18. Natalie Portman is one of my favorite movie stars, but I haven't seen her in any lately.

19. We got to the sailing races just in time to see Jules skipper his in over the finish line.

20. In that math class you have fewer tests.

21. Over the phone they told Peter he had won the raffle.

22. In certain stores in this mall, they always overcharge.

23. You get bored sitting around the house all day.

24. In all of these books they present a true picture of the gypsy life.

25. Maria showed me her butterfly collection and then asked me if I'd like to help her catch one.

MODULE REVIEW

A.   Correcting Faulty Pronoun References in Sentences

Most of the sentences below contain ambiguous, general, indefinite, or weak pronoun references. On your own paper, revise each incorrect sentence. If a sentence is correct, write *C*.

EX.   1.   Paul is older than Luis and Marek, but he is the tallest.

      1.   *Paul is older than Luis and Marek, but Marek is the tallest.*

1. Rita and Pauline met at the shop.

2. Carlos came in first out of a field of five hundred, which is terrific!

3. After we saw a film about the lifestyles of the British royalty, Oscar said he'd like to tour one of them.

4. In some parts of the country, they'll offer a better price for furniture.

5. He was so gullible he believed me no matter which ones I told him.

6. The senator spoke briefly and to the point, which pleased her audience.

7. I couldn't take drama and dance during the same term, so I dropped it.

8. Sondra's mother explained to her why she didn't have time to see the play.

9. At modeling school, you are taught a new way to walk.

10. I really enjoy the science fiction of Arthur C. Clarke, but my brother hasn't read any of them yet.

B.   Proofreading a Paragraph to Correct Faulty Pronoun References

On your own paper, rewrite the following paragraph, correcting any unclear pronoun references. Some sentences may be correct and require no change.

EX.   [1] Since 1924, police have used polygraphs to detect lies, but psychologists still question their reliability.

      [1] *Since 1924, police have used polygraphs to detect lies, but psychologists still question the reliability of the tests.*

[1] The examiner explains to the subject the procedure of the test he is about to take. [2] The subject's wrist and chest are wired to the machine, and this is supposed to measure his emotional responses. [3] Because the subject's pulse, blood pressure, and respiration are unconscious reactions, it's supposed to measure his true feelings.

[4] Examiners require special training before they can give them. [5] Control questions

like "What is your name?" and "Where do you live?" are asked first, and they provide an example of the subject's normal responses. [6] Any unusual movement registered by the polygraph may be a reason to think it's a lie. [7] The examiner tries to ask obvious control questions, but it can't really be scientifically exact. [8] When the examiner studies the results, her judgment depends on how much they differ from what is normal. [9] Since the results depend so much on the abilities of the examiner, they aren't admissible in legal testimony. [10] Therefore, they don't use polygraph test results in courts of law.

C.   Working Cooperatively to Write a Letter to a Celebrity

You have been assigned to write a report on a celebrity of your choice. Work with a partner to write a letter to a celebrity whom you would like to know more about. You might ask the person about his or her accomplishments, goals, family, special training, awards, and childhood. Use at least one pronoun in each of your sentences. Underline the pronouns you use.

EX.

410 W. Evans Ave.
Pittsburgh, PA 15239
September 21, 2018

[Celebrity]
P.O. Box 8950
Hollywood, CA 90027

Dear [Celebrity],

We have been impressed by your active participation in the film industry and would like to know some more about you. For instance, we know you are interested in many issues, one of which is creating a more culturally diverse industry. We would like to know what steps you are taking to help make this happen.

We are also curious about how you manage to be a wife and a mother and a movie star all at the same time. What do think is your most difficult job, and why?

[Celebrity], please write and tell us about yourself. We hope that you are able to accomplish great things and continue to grace our movie screens for a very long time. We hope to meet you one day, and we wish you all the best.

Sincerely yours.
Tama La Croix and April Neiman

REGULAR VERBS

8a The four principal parts of a verb are the *base form*, the *present participle*, the *past*, and the *past participle*. All other forms of the verb are derived from the base form.

EXAMPLES   I **walk** the dog. [base form of *walk*]
I **am walking** the dog. [present participle of *walk*]
I **walked** the dog. [past of *walk*]
I **have walked** the dog. [past participle of *walk*]

8b A *regular verb* is one that forms its past and past participle by adding *–d* or *–ed* to the base form.

Base Form	Present Participle	Past	Past Participle
call	(is) calling	called	(have) called
gnaw	(is) gnawing	gnawed	(have) gnawed
like	(is) liking	liked	(have) liked
paint	(is) painting	painted	(have) painted
tip	(is) tipping	tipped	(have) tipped
watch	(is) watching	watched	(have) watched

NOTE   A few regular verbs have alternate past and past participle forms ending in *–t*. For example, the past and past participle forms of *burn* are *burned* or *burnt*.

When the present participle and the past participle forms are used as main verbs (simple predicates) in sentences, they always require helping verbs.

EXERCISE 1   Writing the Correct Forms of Regular Verbs

For each of the following sentences, decide what the correct form of the italicized verb should be. Write the correct verb form on the line before the sentence.

EX. _____*liked*_____   1. The man *like* his previous job.

_____   1. The kitten purred when Tina *stroke* its head.

_____   2. When Ima is *watch* tennis, she can't hear a word I say.

_____   3. The tiger *jump* over the bar when the lights flickered.

_____   4. My friend is *paint* his bicycle a different color.

_____   5. Most people have *listen* to different types of music on the radio.

_____ 6. The ancient Greeks *pray* to the many gods that they believed in.

_____ 7. I *call* the store for a price, but no one answered the phone.

_____ 8. My dog would have *gnaw* on the bone instead of licking it.

_____ 9. After Jacques left the mall, he *notice* his wallet was missing.

_____ 10. The contestants have *compete* in every possible game show.

_____ 11. Our eleventh-grade chorus is *visit* the local hospital tomorrow.

_____ 12. We have *wait* long enough for the package to arrive.

_____ 13. Payat *poke* his head into the room to tell us dinner was ready.

_____ 14. The city workers have *continue* to search for the hurricane victims.

_____ 15. The car *screech* to a halt when the traffic light changed.

EXERCISE 2   Proofreading Sentences for Correct Verb Forms

In each sentence below, draw a line through any incorrect verb form, and write the correct verb form before the sentence. If a sentence is correct, write *C*.

EX. _____*chewed*_____ 1. Cary ~~chew~~ the crunchy celery.

_____ 1. This tea taste spicy.

_____ 2. Yesterday, we watch a film about the octopus.

_____ 3. Your uncle fix it, but it could break again.

_____ 4. Stephanie greased the axle carefully.

_____ 5. Bill is phone us at the lodge.

_____ 6. Mrs. Vasquez has convince us that she will complete her college education.

_____ 7. Students have perform the dance well this year.

_____ 8. Many chemicals have polluting our rivers and streams.

_____ 9. The museum presenting a large exhibit of African wildlife.

_____ 10. Has the company refund your money?

IRREGULAR VERBS

8c An *irregular verb* forms the past and past participle in some other way than by adding *–d* or *–ed* to the base form.

Base Form	Present Participle	Past	Past Participle
drive	(is) driving	drove	(have) driven
give	(is) giving	gave	(have) given
sing	(is) singing	sang	(have) sung

NOTE   If you are not sure about the principal parts of a verb, look in a dictionary. Entries for irregular verbs give the principal parts.

COMMON IRREGULAR VERBS			
Base Form	**Present Participle**	**Past**	**Past Participle**
be	(is) being	was, were	(have) been
become	(is) becoming	became	(have) become
begin	(is) beginning	began	(have) begun
bite	(is) biting	bit	(have) bitten *or* bit
blow	(is) blowing	blew	(have) blown
break	(is) breaking	broke	(have) broken
bring	(is) bringing	brought	(have) brought
build	(is) building	built	(have) built
burst	(is) bursting	burst	(have) burst
buy	(is) buying	bought	(have) bought
catch	(is) catching	caught	(have) caught
choose	(is) choosing	chose	(have) chosen
come	(is) coming	came	(have) come
cost	(is) costing	cost	(have) cost
do	(is) doing	did	(have) done
draw	(is) drawing	drew	(have) drawn
drink	(is) drinking	drank	(have) drunk
drive	(is) driving	drove	(have) driven
eat	(is) eating	ate	(have) eaten
fall	(is) falling	fell	(have) fallen

COMMON IRREGULAR VERBS

Base Form	Present Participle	Past	Past Participle
feel	(is) feeling	felt	(have) felt
find	(is) finding	found	(have) found
forget	(is) forgetting	forgot	(have) forgotten
freeze	(is) freezing	froze	(have) frozen
get	(is) getting	got	(have) gotten *or* got
give	(is) giving	gave	(have) given
go	(is) going	went	(have) gone
grow	(is) growing	grew	(have) grown
hold	(is) holding	held	(have) held
hurt	(is) hurting	hurt	(have) hurt
keep	(is) keeping	kept	(have) kept
know	(is) knowing	knew	(have) known
lead	(is)leading	led	(have) led
lend	(is) lending	lent	(have) lent
lose	(is) losing	lost	(have) lost
make	(is) making	made	(have) made
meet	(is) meeting	met	(have) met
put	(is) putting	put	(have) put
ride	(is) riding	rode	(have) ridden
ring	(is) ringing	rang	(have) rung
run	(is) running	ran	(have) run
say	(is) saying	said	(have) said
see	(is) seeing	saw	(have) seen
sell	(is) selling	sold	(have) sold
send	(is) sending	sent	(have) sent
show	(is) showing	showed	(have) shown
shrink	(is) shrinking	shrank *or* shrunk	(have) shrunk
sing	(is) singing	sang	(have) sung
sink	(is) sinking	sank *or* sunk	(have) sunk *or* sunken
speak	(is) speaking	spoke	(have) spoken
stand	(is) standing	stood	(have) stood
steal	(is) stealing	stole	(have) stolen
swim	(is) swimming	swam	(have) swum
swing	(is) swinging	swung	(have) swung
take	(is) taking	took	(have) taken
tell	(is) telling	told	(have) told
throw	(is) throwing	threw	(have) thrown
wear	(is) wearing	wore	(have) worn
win	(is) winning	won	(have) won
write	(is) writing	wrote	(have) written

EXERCISE 3 Writing Past and Past Participle Forms of Irregular Verbs

On the line before each sentence, complete the sentences below by writing the correct past or past participle form of the verb in italics.

EX. _____*chose*_____ 1. The woman *choose* her new dress.

_____ 1. The children have *speak* their own languages.

_____ 2. The restaurant has *freeze* the fish for later use.

_____ 3. As a result of too much heat, the clothes have *shrink* in the dryer.

_____ 4. Do you realize that your car tires have *wear* thin?

_____ 5. Last year, many people *become* part of our health care group.

_____ 6. The teacher was so busy that she *forget* to correct the papers.

_____ 7. Once everyone agreed on a time, the people *meet* to resolve the remaining issues.

_____ 8. After Amara had picked a bushel of apples, she picked one for herself and *bite* into it.

_____ 9. The students have *build* a house as a year-long project.

_____ 10. The ancient Romans *get* many of their ideas from Greek culture.

_____ 11. Has everyone *take* her or his shower yet?

_____ 12. Last summer, we *swim* at the YMCA nearly every day.

_____ 13. We *begin* last night's concert with "Respect."

_____ 14. We were disappointed that the store had *sell* all those games.

_____ 15. The phone had *ring* twice by the time I reached it.

_____ 16. The rebel troops had *blow* up the bridge.

_____ 17. Many homes were destroyed when the dam *break*.

_____ 18. Sasha has *keep* busy all morning returning telephone calls.

_____ 19. The audience *leave* quickly after the play was over.

_____ 20. The sunflowers *grow* quite tall last summer.

EXERCISE 4   Proofreading a Paragraph for Past or Past Participle Forms of Verbs

Determine the correct past or past participle form for each of the italicized verbs in the paragraph below. Write the correct form above the verb.

EX.   [1] Ms. Franklin *tell* me about some traditional African sports.
               told

[1] She *say* that wrestling has been practiced in the Sudan for thousands of years.

[2] In the Ethiopian form of wrestling that she saw, young men from different villages *fight* each other. [3] Also in Ethiopia, she was thrilled when teams *ride* horses in the game Feres Gugs. [4] One team chased the other to tag their opponents with wands when the chasers *catch* them. [5] The riders on the opposing team *hold* circular shields to fight off the wands. [6] A spear-throwing competition *be* particularly popular in Uganda and the Democratic Republic of the Congo when she was there. [7] The winner's spear was the one which was *throw* farthest and fastest. [8] Ms. Franklin also has *see* a langa meet in northern Nigeria. [9] The players *run* into each other to try to knock their opponents off balance. [10] She *say* that the sport requires skill, speed, and a good sense of balance.

LIE *AND* LAY

8d The verb *lie* means "to rest," "to recline," or "to remain in a lying position." *Lie* never takes an object. The verb *lay* means "to put (something) in a place." *Lay* usually takes an object.

PRINCIPAL PARTS OF *LIE* AND *LAY*			
Base Form	**Present Participle**	**Past**	**Past Participle**
lie (to rest)	(is) lying	lay	(have) lain
lay (to put)	(is) laying	laid	(have) laid

When deciding whether to use *lie* or *lay*, ask yourself two questions.

Question 1: What do I want to say? Is the meaning "to be in a lying position," or is it "to put something down"?

Question 2: What time does the verb express, and which principal part is used to show this time?

The examples below show how you can apply these questions to determine which verb—*lie* or *lay*—you should use.

EXAMPLE   The cat (*lay, laid*) on the top shelf, hiding.

Question 1: Meaning? The meaning is "to be in a lying position." Therefore, the verb should be *lie*.

Question 2: Principal part? The verb expresses the past, and the sentence requires the past form. The past form of *lie* is *lay*.

ANSWER   The cat **lay** on the top shelf, hiding.

EXERCISE 5   Choosing the Correct Forms of *Lie* and *Lay*

In each of the following sentences, underline the correct form of *lie* or *lay* in parentheses.

EX.   1. The doctor is (*lying, laying*) the instruments on the table.

1. After Robert (*lay, laid*) on the couch, he felt better.
2. When Mother (*laid, lay*) Lana on the quilt, Lana stopped crying.
3. The animals have (*lain, laid*) in the sun for hours.
4. Bricklayers (*lay, lie*) thousands of bricks a year.
5. Where have you (*laid, lain*) the sweater to dry?

6. I would like to (*lay, lie*) my papers over there.

7. (*Lie, Lay*) the box on the dining room table.

8. Have all the students (*laid, lain*) their assignments on the desk?

9. A cloudy mist (*lay, laid*) over the valley.

10. Let's (*lie, lay*) on the beach for a few minutes.

11. The patient is (*lying, laying*) in bed in order to help heal his broken leg.

12. Military officers (*lay, lie*) down rules as helpful guidelines for their troops.

13. He is (*lying, laying*) the new carpet on the floor.

14. Many of the squirrels have (*laid, lain*) acorns beneath the tree.

15. The workers have (*lain, laid*) asphalt the length of the street.

EXERCISE 6   Proofreading Sentences for the Correct Use of *Lie* and *Lay*

In the sentences below, draw a line through each incorrect form of *lie* and *lay*. Write the correct verb form on the line before each sentence. If a sentence is correct, write *C*.

EX. _____*laid*_____ 1. I have ~~lain~~ the blanket on the bed.

_____ 1. After its morning workout, the horse laid in the stall.

_____ 2. The customer is laying his money on the counter.

_____ 3. Be quiet. My mother is laying on the couch.

_____ 4. Khenphet and his brother have lain their coats on the sofa.

_____ 5. Queen bees lay fertilized eggs that will develop into new queens.

_____ 6. The tigers have laid near the water to keep cool.

_____ 7. Monkeys like to lay on the branches of trees.

_____ 8. Please lie my sweater on the railing.

_____ 9. It is difficult to lie tile correctly.

_____ 10. After you have laid in the sun a bit, your swimsuit should be dry.

_____ 11. Yesterday, Sam laid in bed for an hour after the game was over.

_____ 12. Our neighbor is laying in bed, recovering from her illness.

_____ 13. The leather is lying on the rocks to dry.

_____ 14. Lay down in your room before you get too tired.

_____ 15. The father lay his baby in her crib.

SIT *AND* SET *AND* RISE *AND* RAISE

8e The verb *sit* means "to rest in an upright, seated position." *Sit* almost never takes an object. The verb *set* means "to put (something) in a place." *Set* usually takes an object.

PRINCIPAL PARTS OF *SIT* AND *SET*			
Base Form	**Present Participle**	**Past**	**Past Participle**
sit (to rest)	(is) sitting	sat	(have) sat
set (to put)	(is) setting	set	(have) set

EXAMPLES   Please **sit** down.   **Set** it down gently.
                  The vase **sat** on the table.   Don't **set** it there.

8f The verb *rise* means "to go in an upward direction." *Rise* never takes an object. The verb *raise* means "to move (something) in an upward direction." *Raise* usually takes an object.

PRINCIPAL PARTS OF *RISE* AND *RAISE*			
Base Form	**Present Participle**	**Past**	**Past Participle**
rise (to get up)	(is) rising	rose	(have) risen
raise (to lift up)	(is) raising	raised	(have) raised

EXAMPLES   I always **rise** before sunup.
                  Raise that corner just a little more.
                  Bad weather meant food prices **rose** again.
                  Have the grocers **raised** their prices yet?

EXERCISE 7   Proofreading Sentences for Correct Use of *Sit* and *Set* and *Rise* and *Raise*

In the following sentences, draw a line through each incorrect form of *sit, set, rise,* and *raise*. Write the correct verb form on the line before each sentence. If a sentence is correct, write *C*.

EX. _____*sat*_____ 1. The hen ~~set~~ on her eggs.

_____ 1. We didn't want to ~~set~~ down on the damp ground.

_____ 2. The vase of roses is sitting on Mei's desk.

_____ 3. The Mayan farmers rised maize as their primary crop.

_____ 4. Each generation rises its crops a little differently than the previous one.

_____ 5. Ask your brother where he sat the bucket of worms.

_____ 6. Gas prices dropped for a few years and now are raising again.

_____ 7. Some islands in the Pacific are volcanoes that raise up from the ocean floor.

_____ 8. The Pomo basket set in a prominent place.

_____ 9. People the world over have raised sheep for wool.

_____ 10. How would we survive if the sun never raised again?

_____ 11. I could tell that you looked in the trunk because the lid was slightly risen.

_____ 12. The jurors entered the room and set around the table.

_____ 13. If you're tired of standing, set on a folding chair.

_____ 14. The porter has sat your suitcase by the taxi.

_____ 15. Getting a baby to set still for a photograph is no easy job.

_____ 16. Set the piano down gently, please.

_____ 17. Kate had risen her hand and was waving it wildly.

_____ 18. Has the bread raised yet?

_____ 19. We won't leave the tent until the sun has risen.

_____ 20. When Pang heard his name called, he set up straighter.

_____ 21. When Mr. March enters a room, he rises his walking stick and nods.

_____ 22. Steam was rising from the kettle on the stove.

_____ 23. As the lava cools, the ground level actually raises.

_____ 24. I could sit through this film again and again.

_____ 25. If that paper sets in the rain any longer, it will be unreadable.

A. Using the Past and Past Participle Forms of Verbs

On the lines provided, complete the paragraph below by writing the correct past or past participle form of the verb given in parentheses.

EX. [1] Flax has been __*raised*__ *(raise)* for many centuries to make clothes and rope.

[1] People have _____ *(make)* linen, yarn, and rope from flax since at least 8000 B.C. [2] The ancient Egyptians _____ *(wear)* linen clothes and wrapped mummies in linen. [3] Linen cloth _____ *(become)* part of domestic life around the Mediterranean long before the Christian era. [4] Some early linen fabrics _____ *(is)* extremely fine, with five hundred threads to the inch. [5] In the ninth century, Charlemagne _____ *(set)* up centers for linen weaving in Flemish cities. [6] By the late Middle Ages, many Europeans _____ *(weave)* cloth made of wool and linen. [7] At that time, most European monasteries _____ *(produce)* flax for their own use. [8] By the mid-eighteenth century, Ireland had _____ *(become)* a center of linen weaving. [9] The early colonists _____ *(take)* flax with them to North America. [10] A fabric made from linen and wool _____ *(is)* the main clothing material in the colonies.

B. Using the Past and Past Participle Forms Correctly

For each of the following sentences, decide whether the italicized verb is correct. If it is not, write the correct verb form on the line before the sentence. If a sentence is correct, write *C*.

EX. _____*rose*_____ 1. A small tree *raised* up from the rock.

_____ 1. The stock market had *raised.*

_____ 2. Mr. Ito *set* on the board of trustees for the library.

_____ 3. Dr. Johnson has *call* for you twice.

_____ 4. Bright and smooth, the new patchwork quilt *lay* on the sleigh bed.

_____ 5. Surprisingly, silkworms have *became* incapable of surviving on their own in nature.

_____ 6. Without our paddles, we nearly *wash* out to sea during the storm.

_____ 7. You *sample* the eggplant salad for Mother, didn't you?

_____ 8. Where have you *lay* that Russian history book you were reading?

_____ 9. Having a party together nearly *ruin* Shing's and Yori's friendship.

_____ 10. What *happen* during Cinco de Mayo, a Mexican holiday?

C.   Proofreading a Paragraph for the Correct Use of Irregular Verbs

Most of the sentences in the paragraph below contain an error in the use of irregular verbs. Draw a line through each error, and write the correct verb form above the error. Some sentences may have no errors.

forgotten
EX.   [1] In our family, my first camping trip will never be ~~forgot~~.

[1] Lanie and I been seven when we decided to camp near the stream behind my house. [2] We spent an hour setting up the tent about a hundred yards from the house. [3] Lanie had bringed essential supplies of apples and popcorn. [4] My older brother Parnell told us scary stories all evening. [5] Then we gone out with our flashlights to the tent. [6] We made shadows on the tent walls until our batteries run out of power. [7] After we stopped talking, the night sounds taken over. [8] An animal nosing around the tent, probably smelling the popcorn, maked us panic. [9] Be it a skunk or a rat? [10] We wished Lanie had thought fresh batteries were more important than fresh popcorn.

8g The time expressed by a verb is called the *tense* of the verb.

(1) The *present tense* expresses an action (or a state of being) occurring now. The present tense is also used to show a customary or habitual action (or state of being); to convey a general truth, something that is always true; and to summarize the plot or subject matter of a literary work (such use is called the *literary present*).

EXAMPLES   In the evenings, I **run** laps at the track. [customary action]
In "Goldilocks and the Three Bears," a child **learns** about respecting others' privacy and property. [literary present]

(2) The *past tense* expresses an action (or a state of being) that occurred in the past and ended.

EXAMPLE   I **ran** an extra lap last night.

(3) The *future tense* expresses an action (or a state of being) that will occur but has not yet occurred. The future tense is formed with *will* or *shall* and the base form.

EXAMPLE   Next week I **will run** in my first race.

NOTE   A future tense verb may also be expressed by using the present tense of *be* followed by either *going to* or *about to* and the base form of a verb.

EXAMPLES   My best friends **are going to visit** Austin in September.
Dr. Steele **is about to announce** the winner.

(4) The *present perfect tense* expresses an action (or a state of being) that occurred at some indefinite time in the past. The present perfect tense always includes the helping verb *have* or *has*.

EXAMPLE   I **have** not **run** in a race before.

(5) The *past perfect tense* expresses an action (or a state of being) that occurred in the past and was completed before some other past occurrence. The past perfect tense always includes the helping verb *had*.

EXAMPLE   I **had run** for eight months before I decided to enter the race.

(6) The *future perfect tense* expresses an action (or a state of being) that will be completed in the future before some other future occurrence. The future perfect tense always includes the helping verbs *will have* or *shall have*.

EXAMPLE   By the time I leave the track, I **will have run** twelve laps.

Each of the tenses also has a progressive form, which expresses a continuing action (or state of being). It consists of a form of the verb *be* plus the present participle of a verb. The progressive is not a separate tense but an additional form of each of the six tenses.

Form	Examples
Present Progressive	am, is, are running
Past Progressive	was, were running
Future Progressive	will (shall) be running
Present Perfect Progressive	has been, have been running
Past Perfect Progressive	had been running
Future Perfect Progressive	will (shall) have been running

EXERCISE 8   Identifying Verb Tense

For each of the sentences below, identify the tense of the italicized verb. On the line before each sentence, write *pres.* for *present, past* for *past, fut.* for *future, pres. perf.* for *present perfect, past perf.* for *past perfect*, or *fut. perf.* for *future perfect*. Include *prog.* for *progressive form* where appropriate.

EX.   _____past prog._____ 1. George *was trying* to get tickets to the concert.

_____   1. Every month, Virgil *calculates* the interest earned by his savings account.

_____   2. I'm afraid that I *will* never *see* an alien spaceship.

_____   3. The refrigerator *had been running* nonstop for three days.

_____   4. Kuri *brought* home the new <u>Webster's New World Dictionary</u> and <u>Roget's Thesaurus</u>.

_____   5. Kaloma *is* not *carrying* your groceries home again.

_____   6. I *had seen* the amazing running of the athlete at the Olympic Games.

_____   7. *Will* you *have bought* a car by this time next year?

_____   8. Archaeologists *have found* some Mayan temples by studying Landsat photographs from space.

_____   9. Vladimir Nabokov *saw* colors in connection with letters of the alphabet.

_____   10. The waves *have been pounding* this shore for a million years.

SEQUENCE OF TENSES

8h **When describing events that occur at the same time, use verbs in the same tense.**

EXAMPLE   The car **zoomed** by and dust **flew** into the air.

8i **When describing events that occur at different times, use verbs in different tenses to show the order of events.**

EXAMPLE   Kip **plays** the tuba, but years ago he **played** the trumpet. [Kip plays the tuba now, so *plays* is in the present tense. He used to play the trumpet, so *played* is in the past tense.]

8j **Avoid the use of *would have* in "if clauses" that express the earlier of two past actions. Use the past perfect tense.**

NONSTANDARD   If I would have studied more, I would have done better in history.

STANDARD   If I **had studied** more, I would have done better in history.

EXERCISE 9   Using Tenses Correctly

In the sentences below, draw a line through each incorrect verb form, and write the correct form above it.

blew
EX.   1.   Hallie ~~blows~~ the dust off and read the inscription.

1.   The clock fell and breaks into several pieces.

2.   We stand in line forty minutes or so before we could buy tickets.

3.   I had eaten the entire fish before I see the bowls of vegetables.

4.   If I sunk this shot, I will have made nineteen out of twenty.

5.   If the team would have practiced more, it would have won the game.

6.   Have the stores closed for the holiday, or were they open until five?

7.   Lara had sung for sixteen years before she gets her first career break.

8. If you would have closed the window tightly, the rain would not have ruined the wallpaper.

9. Mario hummed softly while he is wrapping up the romano cheese.

10. Because Hans injures his knee, he no longer skates.

8k The *present infinitive* expresses an action (or a state of being) that follows another action or state of being.

EXAMPLE   Julianne wants **to ride** with me. [The action expressed by *to ride* follows the action expressed by *wants*.]

8l The *present perfect infinitive* expresses an action (or a state of being) that comes before another action or state of being.

EXAMPLE   They hoped **to have been** here by now. [The state of being expressed by *to have been* comes before the action expressed by *hoped*.]

8m The *present participle* expresses an action (or a state of being) that occurs at the same time as another action or state of being.

EXAMPLE   **Smiling** through the glass, her mother waved to her. [The action expressed by *Smiling* occurs at the same time as the action expressed by *waved*.]

8n The *present perfect participle* expresses an action (or a state of being) that precedes another action or state of being.

EXAMPLE   **Having finished** his sculpture, he began to clean up. [The action expressed by *Having finished* comes before the action expressed by *began*.]

EXERCISE 10   Revising Sentences for Correct Verb Tense

Draw a line through the incorrect verb forms in the sentences below. On your own paper, write the correct forms above.

to have dropped

EX.   1. The ball signaling the new year was supposed to ~~drop~~ by now.

1. Fighting back a smile, Lucas will give back the toddler's toy.

2. The girls scattered to have hidden from Bernice.

3. Hitting the clock, the startled cat jumped off the mantlepiece.

4. Freyda expected to hand in her resignation by now.

5. Winning the National Book Critics Circle Award, Maxine Hong Kingston became well known for her writings about the Asian American experience.

6. To have sung at the Met is what she wants most of all.

7. Deciding to take a drawing class, Rene registered at the Art Institute.

8. After a tough day like today, it is hard not to have asked, "Why me?"

9. Waiting for the bus yesterday, I nearly freeze.

10. The Luttrells had wanted to have been there by noon.

Voice is the form a transitive verb takes to indicate whether the subject of the verb performs or receives the action.

8o   A verb in the *active voice* expresses an action done by its subject. A verb in the *passive voice* expresses an action done to its subject.

ACTIVE VOICE	Trina and Luis **washed** the car. [The subject, *Trina and Luis*, performed the action.]
PASSIVE VOICE	The car **was washed** by Trina and Luis. [The subject, *car,* received the action.]

A transitive verb in the active voice often has an indirect object as well as a direct object. Either object can become the subject or can remain a complement in the passive construction.

	S V I.O. D.O.
ACTIVE VOICE	Grandpa gave each of us a two-dollar bill.
PASSIVE VOICE	Each of us was given a two-dollar bill (by Grandpa).
PASSIVE VOICE	A two-dollar bill was given to each of us (by Grandpa).

In the preceding examples, the direct object *two-dollar bill* in the active construction becomes the complement in the first passive construction, and the indirect object *each* becomes the subject. In the second passive construction, *two-dollar bill* is the subject, and *each* is the object of the preposition. A complement in a passive construction is called a **retained object**, not a *direct object* or an *indirect object*.

8p   Avoid using the passive voice except in special circumstances.

(1)   Use the passive voice when you do not know who or what performed the action.

EXAMPLES	Did you know that this sweater **was made** by hand?
	I heard that a new bookstore **had been opened** at the mall.

(2)   Use the passive voice when you do not want to reveal who or what performed the action.

EXAMPLES	Many mistakes **were made** in today's game.
	The museum **will be given** one million dollars.

(3)   Use the passive voice when you want to emphasize the receiver of the action.

EXAMPLES	**Were** you absolutely **soaked** by the rain?
	Some fabulous antiques **were found** in the attic.

EXERCISE 11 · Classifying Voice in Sentences

Classify each verb in the sentences below as active or passive. Write *act.* for *active* or *pass.* for *passive* on the line before each sentence.

EX. <u>*act.*</u> 1. The team carried the coach down the field.

_____ 1. Several moths were attracted to the light.

_____ 2. Sometime during the night, the store windows had been broken.

_____ 3. Hortense Powdermaker made connections between psychoanalysis and anthropology.

_____ 4. In the Book of Job, a good man is persecuted for a long time.

_____ 5. Who was handing out pamphlets at the transfer station?

_____ 6. The wet mail was delivered by an equally wet carrier.

_____ 7. You may donate canned goods for the food drive at the supermarket.

_____ 8. The snow will soon be shoveled from the driveway.

_____ 9. The relay team passed the baton smoothly after each lap.

_____ 10. Vivian was singled out for high praise.

EXERCISE 12 · Revising Sentences in the Passive Voice

On your own paper, rewrite each of the sentences below to change passive voice verbs to the active voice.

EX. 1. My newspaper is delivered by a man driving a 1978 Ford.

   1. *A man driving a 1978 Ford delivers my newspaper.*

1. Witch hazel was used by the Cherokees to make a medicinal tea.

2. My lawn mower was tuned up last spring by Emma, who does odd jobs in the neighborhood.

3. The old cellar was filled in by a construction worker driving a bulldozer.

4. After being directed to the ticket office by the conductor, we found our way to the correct gate.

5. Water may be saved by the use of low-flow faucets.

6. Around 1700 B.C., each city of Canaan was ruled by a king.

7. Mary's favorite novels were written by Naguib Mahfouz.

8. When we were overlooked by the host, Bo stepped up and wrote her name on the waiting list.

9. Should laws that apply only to women be written by women?

10. In 1935, the Nobel Prize in chemistry was shared by Frédéric and Irène Joliot-Curie.

Mood is the form a verb takes to indicate the attitude of the person using the verb. Verbs may be in one of three moods: the *indicative*, the *imperative*, or the *subjunctive*.

8q   The *indicative mood* expresses a fact, an opinion, or a question.

EXAMPLES   We **went** to the circus Saturday.
I **think** the clowns were terrific.
Will you come with us next year?

8r   The *imperative mood* expresses a direct command or request.

EXAMPLES   **Get** off my toe!
Hand me that wrench.

8s   The *subjunctive mood* expresses a suggestion, a necessity, a condition contrary to fact, or a wish.

EXAMPLES   It is requested that everyone **arrive** before 9:00 A.M.
If I **were** a sailor, I would sail about Chesapeake Bay.

(1) The *present subjunctive* expresses a suggestion or a necessity.

EXAMPLES   Dad suggested we **build** a TV table.
It is important that I **visit** Aunt Willoughby.

(2) The *past subjunctive* expresses a wish or a condition contrary to fact.

EXAMPLES   I wish I **were** taller.
He bossed us as if he **were** king.

EXERCISE 13   Classifying the Mood of Verbs

Classify the mood for each of the italicized verbs in the following sentences. Write *ind.* for *indicative, imp.* for *imperative,* or *subj.* for *subjunctive* on the line before each sentence.

EX.   __*imp.*__   1. Look out for the boom!

_____   1. If you *were* president, how would you change the budget?

_____   2. The Dorset people *used* stone lamps to light the dark Arctic winters.

_____   3. Please *accept* my apologies for not writing sooner.

_____   4. *Take* two aspirin to ease the pain in your knee.

_____   5. This plane *will take* three hours to get to Dallas.

_____ 6. Our boss insisted that we *wear* safety helmets.

_____ 7. Home to the Algonquian and Athapaskan peoples, the Subarctic *has* always *been* sparsely *populated*.

_____ 8. First, *thread* the needle with fishing line.

_____ 9. Helia guessed that the hummingbirds *migrate* each spring and fall.

_____ 10. It is impossible that Marty *visit* his uncle in Rome.

_____ 11. At that instant, Rosa wished she *were* anyplace else.

_____ 12. If you *do* not *have* a hook and line, you can't go fishing.

_____ 13. Bison *provided* many necessities to the American Indians of the Plains.

_____ 14. Before dinner, *take* this key over to Mercedes' house.

_____ 15. Hoa suggested that I *call* my brother.

_____ 16. *Is* there a word for someone who has lost the sense of smell?

_____ 17. If I *were* the cook, I would add spice to the chili.

_____ 18. Quick, *hand* me the pliers!

_____ 19. Mr. Poe asks that all club members *be* present to vote.

_____ 20. *Listen* carefully; you might learn something.

_____ 21. *Write* your answers on the back of the page.

_____ 22. I should have asked if Yuan *were* the last one on board.

_____ 23. Contrary to common belief, snakes *are* not slimy.

_____ 24. *Try* on this old dress, and take a look in the mirror.

_____ 25. A whippoorwill is a bird that sounds as if it *carries* a megaphone.

MODULE REVIEW

A.   Proofreading Sentences for Correct Verb Usage

Identify the errors in verb usage in each of the sentences below. Draw a line through each incorrect verb form, and write the correct form of the verb above it. Some sentences may be correct.

EX.   1.   Aviva ~~hear~~ *heard* that she got the job.

1.   The two tourists ride the elevator to the seventieth floor and saw the city sparkling below.

2.   Set down on that sofa, and I'll bring you some of my mother's curried eggs.

3.   Ms. Chiago laid the unfinished frame on top of the canvas.

4.   By the time we arrive, I have finished reading your letter.

5.   Chim has worked on that coconut-shell carving since Monday.

6.   Jobelle pumps gas at the crossroads, but last summer she works at the station near Route 60.

7.   If Jacy would have received a scholarship, he would have gone to college.

8.   Around here, the flag is risen at sunup each day.

9.   The receptionist suggested that everyone keeps a schedule on the computer.

10. I wish it were a nice summer day instead of a rainy fall one.

11. We rise in the morning and start on our chores.

12. Since last Monday we have not losed a single game.

13. It looks as though your sari has shrank in the dryer.

14. Lian has studied every night before last week's test, and it showed.

15. Jo is very polite, although he used to have been less courteous.

B. Proofreading a Paragraph for Correct Verb Usage

Identify the errors in verb usage in the following paragraph. Draw a line through each incorrect verb form, and write the correct form of the verb above it. Some sentences may be correct.

were
EX.　[1] Have you ever imagined you ~~are~~ traveling through someone else's body as a microscopic being?

[1] *Fantastic Voyage*, a novel by Isaac Asimov, describe what traveling inside a human might be like. [2] Having liked the book, I decided that I would imagine being inside a jellyfish. [3] This decision may rise a few eyebrows among you readers. [4] However, those of you who have float on an inner tube, pushed along by a mild sea breeze, will understand the idea's appeal. [5] Some jellyfish that drift in tropical seas be so large that I wouldn't have to shrink much to fit inside. [6] Also, some jellyfish are colonies builded of several kinds of members. [7] I hope this spirit of cooperation would allow the colony to temporarily accept a stranger like me. [8] I made up my mind to have spent a quiet day in a tropical jellyfish when an idea striked me. [9] Jellyfish caught smaller animals by stinging them with tentacles. [10] How could I get through the tentacles without being stinged?

C. Writing Notes for a Presentation

You are one of the leaders for a Wilderness Club troop of boys and girls from eleven to twelve years old. You have been asked to give a presentation on first aid at the next meeting. To prepare for your presentation, write your notes so that you can study them.

First, choose an emergency that you could give instructions for, such as a burn, sprain, cut, nosebleed, bee sting, or broken bone. Research the first-aid steps in Red Cross manuals, health books or other reference materials, or on the internet. On your own paper, write the first-aid steps in proper sequence, using complete sentences. Use the active voice, and be sure to use correct verb forms in your sentences.

EX.

First Aid for a Sprained Ankle

The symptoms of a sprained ankle are pain, swelling, and bruising. Start treating a sprained ankle by sponging it with cold water or by applying ice to it. You should wrap the ice in a cloth before putting it on bare skin. After that, wrap the ankle in an elastic bandage to give it support. The bandage manufacturers enclose instructions and diagrams on how to apply these bandages properly. Now, I'll demonstrate how to bandage a sprain.

USES OF MODIFIERS

9a   A *modifier* is a word that limits the meaning of another word. The two kinds of modifiers are *adjectives* and *adverbs*.

(1)   An *adjective* limits the meaning of a noun or a pronoun.

EXAMPLES   **a light** breeze   **an** orangutan   **the best** movie

(2)   An *adverb* limits the meaning of a verb, an adjective, or another adverb.

EXAMPLES   dances **beautifully**   **well** written
exceptionally smart   quite **far**

NOTE   Most modifiers with an *–ly* ending are adverbs. Many adverbs, such as *beautifully* and *hopefully*, are formed by adding *–ly* to adjectives, such as *beautiful* and *hopeful*. However, some modifiers ending in *–ly*, such as *daily* and *early*, may be used as adjectives. A few modifiers, such as *hard, far*, and *long*, have the same form whether used as adjectives or as adverbs.

9b   Use an adjective to modify the subject of a linking verb.

A linking verb is often followed by a **predicate adjective**, a word that modifies the subject.

EXAMPLES   Those sunflowers grew **tall.** [*Tall* follows the linking verb *grew* and modifies the subject, *sunflowers*.]
The accident on the commuter rail was **scary.** [*Scary* follows the linking verb *was* and modifies the subject, *accident*.]

9c   Use an adverb to modify an action verb.

Action verbs are often modified by adverbs that tell *how, when, where,* or *to what extent* an action is performed.

EXAMPLE   The eagle flew **high** above us. [*Flew* is an action verb. The modifiers following it are the adverb *high* and the prepositional phrase *above us*.]

Some verbs, such as *grow, appear, feel, look, sound, smell,* and *taste,* can be used as linking verbs or as action verbs. To determine whether a verb is a linking verb or an action verb, replace the verb with a form of *seem*. If the substitution sounds reasonable, the original verb is a linking verb. If not, it is an action verb.

EXAMPLES   Emilio looked **nervous.** [*Emilio seemed nervous* makes sense. Therefore, *looked* is a linking verb and is modified by the adjective *nervous*.]
Emilio looked **nervously** around the room. [*Emilio seemed nervously around the room* doesn't make sense. Therefore, *looked* is an action verb and is modified by the adverb *nervously*.]

EXERCISE 1   Selecting Modifiers to Complete Sentences

Complete the sentences below by writing appropriate modifiers on the lines provided. In parentheses after the modifier, identify each modifier by writing *adj.* for *adjective* or *adv.* for *adverb*.

EX.   1. Gregory Hines danced   *gracefully (adv.)* .

1. The music is too _____ .

2. Last night we saw a _____ sunset.

3. My neighbor is a _____ talented actress.

4. _____ winds raced through the forest.

5. The kung pao shrimp smells _____ .

6. The algebra test seemed _____ .

7. That wastebasket is _____ full.

8. You look very _____ today.

9. After I read the paper, I cut out a _____ article.

10. The rabbit ran _____ into the thicket.

11. We are _____ coming to the end of this unit of study.

12. The reception for the Japanese authors was _____ planned.

13. The pole-vaulter leaped _____ and cleared the beam.

14. Do you know all the words to this _____ song?

15. "I'm not wearing that _____ costume!" Ben shouted.

MODULE 9: CORRECT USE OF MODIFIERS

SIX TROUBLESOME MODIFIERS

9d   *Bad* **is an adjective.** *Badly* **is an adverb. In standard English, only the adjective form should follow a linking verb.**

NONSTANDARD   If the punch tastes badly, we'll have to make some more.

STANDARD   If the punch tastes **bad,** we'll have to make some more.

9e   *Good* **is an adjective.** *Well* **may be used as an adjective or as an adverb. Avoid using** *good* **to modify an action verb. Use** *well* **as an adverb meaning "capably" or "satisfactorily." As an adjective,** *well* **means "in good health" or "satisfactory in appearance or condition."**

NONSTANDARD   Conchetta sings very good, don't you think?

STANDARD   Conchetta sings very **well,** don't you think?

STANDARD   After taking the medicine given him by the doctor, Mario felt **well** again.

9f   *Slow* **is an adjective.** *Slowly* **is an adverb. Avoid the common error of using** *slow* **to modify an action verb.**

NONSTANDARD   The waiter moved so slow that we thought he must be extremely tired.

STANDARD   The waiter moved so **slowly** that we thought he must be extremely tired.

EXERCISE 2   Choosing Correct Modifiers

In the following sentences, underline the correct modifier in parentheses.

EX.   1.   Isobella looks (*good, well*) with her new hairdo.

1.   Turtles and snails are two animals that move rather (*slow, slowly*).

2.   Don't feel (*bad, badly*) if you lose the game; just play as hard as you can.

3.   The artist Monet had an unusually (*good, well*) eye for light and shadows.

4.   Harley didn't feel (*good, well*), so he went to see the school nurse.

5.   This bus is quite (*slow, slowly*) because it stops at almost every corner.

6.   Some young players have difficulty learning to be (*good, well*) losers.

7.   I'm afraid I sang that song (*bad, badly*); may I try again?

Houghton Mifflin Harcourt Publishing Company   141   Module 9

8. The truck went (*slow, slowly*) down the icy hill.

9. The sauce tasted (*good, well*) after Ramon added a little parsley.

10. The special effects were done so (*good, well*) that the alien spaceship seemed totally realistic.

11. The car drove (*good, well*) after Regina had the tires rotated.

12. When I was baby-sitting, little Peter was cheerful, but his sister acted (*bad, badly*) all afternoon.

13. The honey oozed out of the bottle (*slow, slowly*).

14. "I don't know my lines (*good, well*) enough yet," the actor admitted.

15. The cat crept (*slow, slowly*) along the path, watching the birds.

16. "Drive (*slow, slowly*) so that we don't miss our turn," Al said.

17. Don't eat the fruit if it is (*bad, badly*).

18. Ever since Helena moved away, Emma has missed her (*bad, badly*).

19. If the next song is a (*slow, slowly*) one, I hope that Ossie asks me to dance.

20. Marissa paints as (*good, well*) as a professional artist.

21. We'll win today's game if our luck continues to be (*good, well*).

22. Without enough sun or water, the plants suffered (*bad, badly*).

23. Do you think that this perfume smells (*good, well*)?

24. "You will look (*good, well*) again once the marks from the chickenpox fade," the doctor assured the young boy.

25. The day at the beach passed (*slow, slowly*), and we finished our books.

COMPARISON OF MODIFIERS

9g *Comparison* **refers to the change in the form of an adjective or an adverb to show increasing or decreasing degrees in the quality that the modifier expresses.**

There are three degrees of comparison: *positive, comparative*, and *superlative*. The **positive degree** of a modifier is used to modify a single thing. The **comparative degree** is used to describe one of two things. The **superlative degree** is used to describe one of three or more things.

POSITIVE   Nico keeps his room **neat.**
COMPARATIVE   Nico's room is **neater** than Susan's.
SUPERLATIVE   Nico's room is the **neatest** one in the whole house.

(1) Most one-syllable modifiers form the comparative and superlative degrees by adding *–er* and *–est.*

EXAMPLE   The gray horse is **fast,** the black one is **faster,** and the white one is the **fastest** of all.

(2) Some two-syllable modifiers form the comparative and superlative degrees by adding *–er* and *–est.* Other two-syllable modifiers form the comparative and superlative degrees by using *most* and *more.*

Positive	Comparative	Superlative
simple	simpler	simplest
freely	more freely	most freely

(3) Modifiers of more than two syllables form the comparative and superlative degrees by using *more* and *most.*

Positive	Comparative	Superlative
efficient	more efficient	most efficient
skillfully	more skillfully	most skillfully

(4) To show a decrease in the qualities they express, all modifiers form the comparative and superlative degrees by using *less* and *least.*

Positive	Comparative	Superlative
proud	less proud	least proud
reasonably	less reasonably	least reasonably

(5) Some modifiers do not follow the regular methods of forming the comparative and superlative degrees.

Positive	Comparative	Superlative
bad	worse	worst
well/good	better	best
many/much	more	most
little	less	least

EXERCISE 3   Forming the Degrees of Comparison of Modifiers

On your own paper, write the forms for the comparative and superlative degrees of the following modifiers. Write the comparative and superlative degrees with *less* and *least*, too.

EX.   1. happily   *more (less) happily, most (least) happily*
        2. slow   *slower, less slow; slowest, least slow*

1. carefully
2. importantly
3. quick
4. beautiful
5. joyful
6. tall
7. lazy
8. fashionable
9. terrifically
10. soothing
11. loudly
12. easy
13. sincere
14. nervous
15. hungry
16. absent-minded
17. direct
18. clearly
19. brave
20. grainy

EXERCISE 4   Using Comparison Forms of Adjectives

On your own paper, write a sentence comparing each of the pairs below. Use the comparative form of adjectives in your sentences.

EX.   1. the sun and the moon
        The sun is larger than the moon.

1. summer and winter
2. writing and revising
3. movies and television
4. dogs and cats
5. sandals and moccasins
6. lying and telling the truth
7. ice-skating and roller-skating
8. mountain climbing and spelunking
9. computer games and board games
10. plastic flowers and real flowers

MODULE 9: CORRECT USE OF MODIFIERS

USES OF COMPARATIVE AND SUPERLATIVE FORMS

9h **Use the comparative degree when comparing two things. Use the superlative degree when comparing more than two.**

COMPARATIVE This computer is **faster** than that one.
Of the two players, Paco is the **more skillful.**
This sound system is **less expensive** than yours was.

SUPERLATIVE This computer is the **fastest** of all the models on the market.
Of the three players, Paco is the **most skillful.**
This sound system is the **least expensive** one of those I have seen.

NOTE In everyday conversation, people sometimes use the superlative degree in comparing two things: *Put your best foot forward.* In your writing, however, you should use the comparative degree when comparing two things.

9i **Include the word** *other* **or** *else* **when comparing one thing with others in the same group.**

NONSTANDARD Andrea can sing better than anyone in the choir. [Andrea cannot sing better than herself.]

STANDARD Andrea can sing better than **anyone else** in the choir.

9j **Avoid double comparisons. A double comparison is incorrect because it contains both** *-er* **and** *more* **(or** *less***) or** *-est* **and** *most* **(or** *least***).**

NONSTANDARD The first book was more longer than the second one was.
STANDARD The first book was **longer** than the second one was.
NONSTANDARD What state has the most coldest weather?
STANDARD What state has the **coldest** weather?

EXERCISE 5   Revising Sentences by Correcting Modifiers

In each of the following sentences, draw a line through the incorrect modifiers. On the line before each sentence, write the correct comparative or superlative form. Write *C* if the sentence is correct.

EX. _____*sicker*_____ 1. The doctor was ~~more sicker~~ than I was.

_____ 1. Great Danes are more bigger than collies.

_____ 2. This is the most best grapefruit that I have ever tasted.

_____ 3. Of all the planets, Mercury is closer to the sun.

_____ 4. In your opinion, who is the most fastest athlete today?

_____ 5. Georgio's joke was most humorous than mine.

_____ 6. To me, a poem is harder to write than any piece of literature I have attempted.

_____ 7. Mama's roghan josh is less spicier than Grandma's.

_____ 8. Which country has the largest population, China or India?

_____ 9. Out of all the contest entries, yours was better.

_____ 10. This TV is the least expensive one in the store.

_____ 11. Texas is more larger than any other state, except Alaska.

_____ 12. He felt least enthusiastic before the game than he did once the Phillies got a home run.

_____ 13. Of all the movies I've seen, this one was the absolute worse for dialogue.

_____ 14. I think you need to try on a more smaller size; those shoes are too loose.

_____ 15. The climate of Maine is least warm than that of Florida.

_____ 16. Are pigs really more smarter than dogs?

_____ 17. I think Amsterdam is more beautiful than any city I have visited in the world.

_____ 18. She found rugby more challenging than lacrosse.

_____ 19. Of the Jewish holy days, Yom Kippur is one of the more important.

_____ 20. The new monorail travels most quickly than the old train.

_____ 21. It is more easier to get there than to get back.

_____ 22. Winter is the most bad time to visit Sven.

_____ 23. I like the desert more better than Louis does.

_____ 24. Their house is the most colorful on the block.

_____ 25. Who spoke most eloquently, Paula or Abraham?

MODULE 9: CORRECT USE OF MODIFIERS
MODULE REVIEW

A. Using Modifiers Correctly

In the sentences below, draw a line through each incorrect modifier. Write the correct modifier on the line before the sentence. If a sentence is correct, write *C*.

EX. _____*best*_____ 1. Of all the Dutch cities, Leiden is probably the ~~better~~ one to visit if you want to see fields of tulips.

_____ 1. In the sixteenth century, Carolus Clusius brought the most earliest tulip bulb to the Netherlands from Turkey.

_____ 2. Ever since then, tulips have grown good in the Netherlands.

_____ 3. Today, tulips are among the Netherlands' most biggest exports.

_____ 4. They also happen to be one of the country's popularest tourist attractions.

_____ 5. Naturally, of all the seasons, spring is the better time to visit if you want to see flowers.

_____ 6. One of the easiest ways to see the tulips is to ride the train.

_____ 7. As the train passes slow through Leiden, you can see the vast tulip fields.

_____ 8. The fields look well, covered with blocks of flowers in many vivid colors.

_____ 9. Near Leiden, farther west, are the most largest flower gardens in the world.

_____ 10. Named the Keukenhof Gardens, they are truly beautifully.

_____ 11. You'd feel badly if you went all the way to Leiden and failed to see them.

_____ 12. More flowers grow there than in any garden in the world.

_____ 13. Tulips bloom more later in the spring than some other flowers.

_____ 14. More earlier in the year, daffodils and hyacinths bloom.

_____ 15. Of the three kinds of flowers, I feel the tulips are the more dramatic.

B. Proofreading a Paragraph for Correct Use of Modifiers

In the paragraph below, draw a line through each incorrect modifier. Write the correct modifier above the error. Some sentences have no errors.

EX. [1] The city of Honfleur lies ~~quiet~~ *quietly* on the coast of Normandy, a region in northern France.

[1] Unlike Le Havre, a much largest city nearby, Honfleur looks like a fishing village of long ago. [2] Honfleur is the birthplace of Erik Satie, one of the more creative composers who ever lived. [3] In the early 1900s, Satie wrote least complicated music than other composers wrote. [4] Satie wrote long ballet scores and more shorter pieces for the piano. [5] He also worked as a pianist in Paris, France's capital and larger city. [6] His critics treated him badly. [7] Perhaps critics would have treated Satie more kinder if he hadn't given his pieces such strange names. [8] One of his most earliest works was called *Truly Flabby Preludes for a Dog.* [9] He wrote even more humorouser performance directions. [10] Of all of them, the most funniest was "to be played like a nightingale with a toothache."

C. Writing a Memo

You are on the staff of a major television network. You must decide which two of the four possible new series below you will recommend for the new fall season. On your own paper, write a memo of at least ten sentences to your boss, explaining the reasons for your choices. Use modifiers correctly to explain your choices.

1. *Space Pioneers:* a series about such prominent figures as Russian cosmonaut Yuri Gagarin, the first person in space, and American astronaut Mae C. Jemison, the first African American female in space
2. *Strange Pets:* a series about famous people and their strange pets. First episode: Abraham Lincoln and his White House pet, a turkey named Jack
3. *Deep Trouble:* a comedy about a modern family that lives on a submarine
4. *A Stitch in Time:* a science fiction adventure about a tailor who journeys to other time periods, both historic and futuristic

EX.   *To: Iris Shaw, Program Manager*

From: *Charles Mills, Program Assistant*

Date: *October 21, 2008*

Re: *Fall season recommendations*

One of the most popular topics today is space travel. For this and other reasons, I think Space Pioneers is a good choice for a new series.

MISPLACED MODIFIERS

A modifying phrase or clause that sounds awkward because it modifies the wrong word or group of words is called a *misplaced modifier.*

10a   Avoid using a misplaced modifier.

To correct a misplaced modifier, place the phrase or clause as close as possible to the word or words you intend it to modify.

MISPLACED   Ms. Sims saw the cat jump off the roof while gardening.

   CLEAR   **While gardening,** Ms. Sims saw the cat jump off the roof.

10b   Avoid placing a phrase or clause so that it seems to modify either of two words. Such a misplaced modifier is often called a *two-way,* or *squinting, modifier.*

MISPLACED   The teacher said when class met she would explain the talent contest.

   CLEAR   **When class met,** the teacher said she would explain the talent contest.

   CLEAR   The teacher said she would explain the talent contest **when class met.**

EXERCISE 1   Revising Sentences by Correcting Misplaced or Squinting Modifiers

Revise each of the following sentences by underlining the misplaced or squinting modifier. Then insert a caret ($\wedge$) to show where the modifier should be placed.

EX.   1. $\wedge$ We stopped to see the quaint old house <u>on the way to school</u>.

1. My friend said during intermission she almost always liked comedies.

2. The tired explorers noticed a herd of elephants eating as they rode their jeeps across the savannah.

3. Emily and Jenny overheard the aliens planning a surprise attack on the roof today.

4. Carlos and I listened intently to the commentator on the radio drinking lemonade.

5. There is a watch in the dresser upstairs that is over fifty years old.

6. Returning home on the ferry, a whale was seen by the tourists.

7. The legislator running for reelection last night admitted in his speech he had made some mistakes.

8. Tamara decided she'd like to visit the West Indies while reading a brochure.

9. The circus was quite exciting, but I watched the motorcyclists crossing the high wire nervously.

10. The teacher asked Bill after class to take another exam.

11. Every morning, Carrie made certain she fed her pet goldfish wanting to be responsible.

12. To do all sorts of interesting tricks, Don liked to hire magicians for the entertainment of his party guests.

13. Rita promised when it started to snow she would buy a new winter coat and mittens.

14. They were silent as they witnessed the northern lights sitting on their porch.

15. After lifting weights for six months, we noticed that Kiyoshi had some new muscles.

16. I agreed on Tuesday I would help Sheila.

17. The lifeguard made sure to tell the swimmers to get out of the water before taking a break.

18. Shimmering in the golden afternoon sunlight, the vacationers enjoyed the view of the city.

19. The cowhands wondered on the second night of the cattle drive where fifteen steers went.

20. Joachim had finally learned how to do a double-flip off the high board bursting with pride.

21. Don't forget to write every point of the treaty down on paper that will end this conflict.

22. Tell your sister before she leaves for the party I need to see her.

23. We were amazed after we read we had passed our exams with all A's on the bulletin board.

24. The men crossing the desert on foot were grateful when they encountered the merchants, having empty canteens.

25. The wind blew down the fence that reached a speed of fifty miles per hour.

DANGLING MODIFIERS

A modifying phrase or clause that does not sensibly modify any word or words in a sentence is called a *dangling modifier.*

10c   Avoid using a dangling modifier.

You may correct a dangling modifier in one of two ways.

(1) Add a word or words that the phrase or clause can sensibly modify.

(2) Add a word or words to the phrase or clause itself.

DANGLING   Handing out papers, the teacher's pencil slipped from her hand.
[Whose hand was it?]

CLEAR   **Handing out papers,** the teacher let her pencil slip from her hand.

DANGLING   After climbing to the mountaintop, it was too cloudy to see very far.
[Who was climbing?]

CLEAR   **After climbing to the mountaintop,** we found that the weather was too cloudy to allow us to see very far.

DANGLING   While working at the shop, news arrived of his brother's wedding.
[Was the news working at the shop?]

CLEAR   **While Alejandro was working at the shop,** news arrived of his brother's wedding.

NOTE   A few dangling modifiers have become standard in idiomatic expressions.

EXAMPLES   **Generally speaking,** it doesn't snow here until mid-to-late February.

To be perfectly frank, the speech was quite dull.

EXERCISE 2   Revising Sentences by Correcting Dangling Modifiers

On your own paper, revise each sentence to eliminate the dangling modifier.

EX.   1.   After four days of camping, the home-cooked meal tasted great.

1.   *After four days of camping, the boys thought the home-cooked meal tasted great.*

1.   Having purchased fishing equipment, a trip to the lake was taken.

2.   Before calling 911, a house that is on fire should be vacated immediately.

3.   Thrilled by all the attention, Sallie's face lit up in a smile.

4. The sound of many cars honking their horns was heard while making a slow left turn.

5. To earn a place in the school orchestra, daily practice is necessary.

6. While waiting for the phone to ring, an interesting program was on television.

7. Relaxing on the beach, dark storm clouds appeared.

8. Surprised by the sudden sound of the alarm, the rescue trucks were hastily driven to the scene of the accident.

9. For the benefit of the audience, replacing the old seats was his first task as theater manager.

10. To help the candidate win the election, many signs must be made.

11. After sitting in the sun for a while, the lotion was applied.

12. Driving the boat too fast, from shore Dad shouted at me to slow down.

13. Before leaving town, the hotel bill needed to be paid.

14. Encouraged by the favorable reviews his first play received, another one was written almost immediately.

15. While making room on the desk for the new computer, the box of pencils fell to the floor.

EXERCISE 3   Writing Sentences with Modifiers

On your own paper, write complete sentences, using each of the modifiers given below as the introductory element of the sentence. To be sure you include a word or words the modifier can sensibly refer to, underline the word or words modified.

EX. 1. after class
     1. *After class, we all walked to the store.*

1. before practicing the piano
2. jumping high into the air
3. delighted by the beautiful weather
4. to help his brother understand the problem better
5. while rummaging through the basement
6. after years of hard work
7. filled with pride
8. having read the article
9. skating circles around Fred
10. laughing softly

A.   Revising Sentences by Correcting Misplaced Modifiers

For each of the sentences below, underline the misplaced or squinting modifier. Then insert a caret (∧) to show where the modifier should be placed.

EX.   1.   ∧We saw it was going to be quite a year for sports <u>reading our school newspaper</u>.

1.   My brother Carlos assured me after breakfast the school was going to be a contender in almost every sport.

2.   Sometime in the spring the paper said that Pearl Chen, last year's shot put champion, will be trying out for the nationals.

3.   My brother said we had to be at every football game right after reading the article.

4.   We remembered when the coach told the fullback he would have to play on both defense and offense in the middle of the Glendale game.

5.   This year the paper informed us there is a new person playing fullback.

6.   The article talked about Chris Evler which was very positive.

7.   Carlos said during the season that the new fullback would probably win several awards.

8.   We were happy to see the girl's hockey team practicing on the way to school.

9.   Carlos and I watched Ingrid Swanson make a tricky goal while walking through the park.

10.   We lingered by the rink to watch the game admiring Ingrid's skill.

11.   Carlos reminded me the sports writers had predicted that the basketball team would be state champions for two more years right after last spring's playoffs.

12.   Carlos, who played center on the team, was waiting for the basketball season to begin quite impatiently.

13.   Carlos had often told me on the basketball court anyone can figure out how to pass and shoot the ball.

14.   What makes the game interesting is that one player has to outmanuever the other player while trying to make a basket.

15.   I finally admitted to Carlos that after the baseball season began I would be happy.

B. Revising Sentences by Correcting Dangling Modifiers

On your own paper, rewrite each sentence to correct the dangling modifier.

EX. 1. Having seen *Superman: The Movie*, it was amazing how Christopher Reeve, playing Superman, could perform all those incredible acts.

1. *Having seen <u>Superman: The Movie,</u> we were amazed at the way Christopher Reeve, playing Superman, could perform all those incredible acts.*

1. To make a good fantasy like *Superman: The Movie*, solutions to technical problems must be provided.
2. Suspended by two wires from a pole, the flying really seems to occur.
3. Photographers sometimes tried trick photography using models of New York City's streets.
4. Superman's cape swirled in the wind which was operated by remote control.
5. To keep Reeve from crashing into the studio wall, a net was placed at the end of the track.
6. The director said it is difficult to create the effect of a character flying after working with *Superman: The Movie*.
7. When creating animated films, fantastic scenes are as easy to draw as ordinary scenes.
8. When shoving a big boulder off a mountain, however, it must be played by a real person.
9. The boulder and the mountain were built in miniature size on which it stood.
10. Thinking that Superman was really standing on the mountain, the final scene was quite effective.

C. Collaborating to Write a Story Starter

You and a partner are writing a science fiction story. As prewriting, you have jotted down the phrases and clauses below. On your own paper, work together to use five phrases or clauses to begin the story. Make sure that you don't have any dangling or misplaced modifiers.

EX. speeding through the galaxy at a breakneck speed
Speeding through the galaxy at a breakneck speed, the crew suddenly noticed the ship was running low on rocket fuel.

landing with a bump on the distant planet
to make sure the pressure suits contained enough oxygen
after checking for alien life forms
before reaching for her laser rifle
having an extremely large head and what seemed to be a purple tail
running out of food
boasting that he knew better than the rest how to survive in space
relieved when they saw the strange, blue sun vanish from the screen
while it sounded like a meteorite had hit the hull
turning to face them with a grim expression

AFFECT / BEING AS, BEING THAT

This module contains a **glossary,** or alphabetical list, of common problems in English usage. Throughout the module, examples are labeled *standard* or *nonstandard*. **Standard English** is the most widely accepted form of English. **Nonstandard English** is language that does not follow the rules and guidelines of standard English.

affect, effect *Affect* is a verb meaning "to influence." *Effect* used as a verb means "to bring about." Used as a noun, *effect* means "the result of some action."

EXAMPLES   Years of playing in a rock-and-roll band **affected** Brian's hearing.
The principal has **effected** changes in lunchroom schedules.
The medicine had no **effect** on my cold.

all the farther, all the faster Avoid these expressions. Use *as far as* and *as fast as*.

NONSTANDARD   Eighty miles per hour is all the faster that electric car can go.
STANDARD   Eighty miles per hour is **as fast as** that electric car can go.

allusion, illusion An *allusion* is a reference to something. An *illusion* is a mistaken idea or a misleading appearance.

EXAMPLES   Literature is full of **allusions** to the Bible and to Shakespeare.
This book of magic tricks will teach you how to create many popular **illusions.**

alumni, alumnae *Alumni* is the plural of *alumnus* (a male graduate). *Alumnae* is the plural of *alumna* (a female graduate). As a group, the graduates of a coeducational school are usually called *alumni*.

EXAMPLES   The women's college planned a conference for its **alumnae.**
All of these **alumni** were once members of the men's chorus.
Alumni often wear T-shirts with their colleges' names on them.

NOTE   In informal usage the graduates of a women's college may be called *alumni*. However, *alumnae* is preferred in formal situations.

anyways, anywheres, everywheres, nowheres, somewheres Use these words without the *s* at the end.

EXAMPLE   We couldn't find the keys **anywhere.**

as, as if   See **like, as, as if**.
at   Do not use *at* after *where*.

EXAMPLE   Where did you find Tanya? [not *find Tanya at*]
               In formal situations, do not use the construction *reason ... is because*.
Instead, use *reason ... is that*.

NONSTANDARD   The reason for the ordinance against washing cars is because we have
               a water shortage.
   STANDARD   The **reason** for the ordinance against washing cars **is that** we have a
               water shortage.

being as, being that   Avoid using these expressions. Use *because* or *since* instead.

NONSTANDARD   Being as Carol was the best candidate, we voted for her.
   STANDARD   **Because** Carol was the best candidate, we voted for her.

EXERCISE 1   Identifying Correct Usage

For each sentence below, underline the correct word or words in parentheses.

> EX.   1.   Your shoe is (*somewheres*, <u>*somewhere*</u>) in the living room.

1.   The sad song on his latest album (*affected, effected*) my mood.
2.   (*Being as, Because*) Lawrence draws well, we had him design the brochure.
3.   The colors on my wall were part of an optical (*allusion, illusion*).
4.   The reason for playing soft music is (*because, that*) customers like it.
5.   That bad weather had an (*affect, effect*) on my driving.
6.   Three hundred miles is (*all the farther, as far as*) I can travel.
7.   The (*effect, affect*) of the changes in the test schedule was obvious.
8.   Where is that (*puppy at, puppy*)?
9.   Joaquin made (*allusions, illusions*) to his favorite stories in that essay.
10. Zora looked (*everywheres, everywhere*) for her keys.
11. Franklin Roosevelt's New Deal (*affected, effected*) great changes in the United
     States.
12. The (*alumni, alumnae*), both men and women, donated money for a women's
     studies center.
13. Thirty miles an hour was (*all the faster, as fast as*) the train could travel.
14. (*Being that, Because*) we were tired, we called it a night.
15. The (*alumni, alumnae*) of the girls' school all went to college.

COULD OF / OFF, OFF OF

could of   Do not use *of* with the helping verb *could*. Use *have* instead. Also avoid *had of, ought to of, should of, would of, might of,* and *must of.*

EXAMPLE   I **could have** been a contender. [not *could of*]

effect, affect   See **affect.**

emigrate, immigrate *Emigrate* means "to leave a country or region to settle elsewhere." *Immigrate* means "to come into a country or region to settle there." Remember that *emigrate* always takes *from* and *immigrate* always takes *to.*

EXAMPLES   How many people have **emigrated** from Ireland?
Many Irish **immigrated** to Boston.

everywheres   See **anyways,** etc.

he, she, it, they   Avoid using a pronoun along with its antecedent as the subject of a verb.

NONSTANDARD   My brother, he won the fifty-yard dash.
   STANDARD   My **brother** won the fifty-yard dash.

illusion   See **allusion.**

kind of, sort of   In formal situations, avoid using *kind of* for the adverb *somewhat* or *rather.*

INFORMAL   Otto was kind of unhappy when he did not make the swimming team.
   FORMAL   Otto was **somewhat** [or **rather**] unhappy when he did not make the swimming team.

kind of a, sort of a   In formal situations, omit the *a.*

INFORMAL   What kind of a pet would you like?
   FORMAL   What **kind of** pet would you like?

like, as, as if   *Like* is a preposition. In formal situations, do not use *like* for the conjunctions *as, as if,* or *as though* to introduce a subordinate clause.

INFORMAL   You look like you need some help.
   FORMAL   You look **as if** [or **as though**] you need some help.

nowheres   See **anyways,** etc.

off, off of   Do not use *off* or *off of* in place of *from.*

NONSTANDARD	You can get a train schedule off of that conductor.
STANDARD	You can get a train schedule **from** that conductor.

EXERCISE 2 Identifying Correct Usage

For each sentence below, underline the correct word or words in parentheses.

EX.   1. Leslie (*could of, could have*) helped you with your project.

1. My ancestors (*emigrated, immigrated*) from Italy many years ago.
2. Gina was (*kind of, somewhat*) unhappy that she did not receive a part in the play.
3. It looks (*like, as if*) we'll go to the grand opening of the mall.
4. My friend Kayla (*isn't, she isn't*) happy about the plan to move her desk across the room.
5. Did you buy a stamp (*from, off*) the woman at the post office on Main Street?
6. I would like to formally introduce Delia, who plays her violin (*as, like*) a professional does.
7. The evening bus for commuters is usually (*sort of, rather*) crowded.
8. You (*might have, might of*) warned me about this problem.
9. Did you receive an invitation (*off of, from*) Elsie?
10. If you want to learn the basics about computers, it doesn't matter what (*kind of a, kind of*) computer you have.

EXERCISE 3 Proofreading a Paragraph to Correct Usage Errors

For each sentence in the paragraph below, draw a line through the error in usage. Then write the correct usage in the space above each word.

EX.   [1] I could not *~~of~~* picked a more interesting topic for my report.
have

[1] I borrowed off of the town library a science book that describes this kind of insect. [2] As you might of guessed, moths and butterflies are related but difficult to tell apart. [3] However, this book, it says that moths usually fly around in the evening and at night, while butterflies are usually seen in the daytime. [4] When resting on a plant, moths don't hold their wings upright like butterflies do; instead, they lay their

wings down flat. [5] It is sort of fascinating to learn that there are over 100,000 kinds

of moths but only 17,000 types of butterflies.

MODULE 11: A GLOSSARY OF USAGE

OR, NOR / WHO, WHOM, WHICH, THAT

or, nor   Use *or* with *either;* use *nor* with *neither.*

EXAMPLES   We can **either** go to a movie **or** simply walk in the park.
Neither Alexandra **nor** Alfonso will forget to deliver the important package.

reason ... is because   See **because.**

some, somewhat   Use *somewhat* to mean "to some extent."

INFORMAL   After reading the long letter, Karl's mood brightened **some.**

FORMAL   After reading the long letter, Karl's mood brightened **somewhat.**

somewheres   See **anyways,** etc.

sort of   See **kind of.**

sort of a   See **kind of a.**

than, then   *Than* is a conjunction used in comparisons. *Then* is an adverb telling when.

EXAMPLES   I don't know anyone who sleeps more soundly **than** I do.
The violinist tightened the bow, **then** tuned the strings.

this here, that there   Avoid using *here* or *there* after *this* or *that.*

EXAMPLE   **That** automobile looks like a June bug [not *That there*]

type, type of   Avoid using *type* as an adjective. Add *of* after *type.*

NONSTANDARD   Cherese, do you still prefer this type running shoe to the other type?

STANDARD   Cherese, do you still prefer this **type of** running shoe to the other type?

when, where   Do not use *when* or *where* to begin a definition.

NONSTANDARD   Alliteration is when the beginning sounds of words are repeated.

STANDARD   Alliteration is **a figure of speech in which** the beginning sounds of words are repeated.

NONSTANDARD   Estimating is where you make a guess about the size or quantity of something.

STANDARD   Estimating is **a problem-solving technique** used to guess the size or quantity of something.

who, whom, which, that   *Who* and *whom* refer to persons only. *Which* refers to things only. *That* may refer to either persons or things.

EXAMPLES   Was it Don Marquis **who** wrote "The Lesson of the Moth"?
That poem, **which** appears in the book *Archy and Mehitabel,* is one of my favorites.
It is a poem **that** I think about often.
The person **that** showed me the poem was Kimberly.

EXERCISE 4   Identifying Correct Usage

For each sentence below, underline the correct word or words in parentheses.

EX.   1. After the training session, the puppy's behavior improved (*some,* *somewhat*).

1. Neither Pedro (*or, nor*) Collin feels strongly about the issue.
2. Who can run that race faster (*than, then*) Marlena can?
3. That (*type, type of*) guitar is quite expensive.
4. The woman (*who, which*) painted our house did a wonderful job.
5. Aponi shucked the corn and (*then, than*) filled a pot with water.
6. Please call either Jason (*nor, or*) Pauli as soon as possible.
7. The wind died down (*somewhat, some*), so cycling was easier.
8. A collage (*is when a person pastes, involves pasting*) different objects and papers together to form a picture.
9. Mary watered (*that, that there*) garden yesterday afternoon.
10. The window screen, (*which, who*) ripped in the storm, is being replaced.

EXERCISE 5   Proofreading a Paragraph to Correct Usage Errors

In the sentences below, draw a line through each error in usage. Then write the correct usage in the space above the word. Some sentences may be correct.

        That
EX.   [1] ~~That there~~ table in the library is made out of marble.

[1] Marble is when limestone is compressed and made very hot. [2] This here rock

in its purest form is white. [3] Most marble has either one substance nor another in it that gives it different colors. [4] Because it is somewhat easy to shape, marble is often

used for statues. [5] The best type sculpting marble comes from Italy.

THE DOUBLE NEGATIVE

A *double negative* is a construction in which two or more negative words are used where one is enough.

NONSTANDARD	Herbert never has no time to relax any more.
STANDARD	Herbert **never** has time to relax any more.

or

Herbert has **no** time to relax any more.

the contraction *n't*   Do not use the contraction *n't,* meaning *not,* with another negative word.

NONSTANDARD	There isn't no tread on those tires.
STANDARD	There isn't **any** tread on those tires.

barely, hardly, scarcely   Do not use *barely, hardly,* or *scarcely* with another negative word.

NONSTANDARD	There aren't hardly any tickets left for the concert.
STANDARD	There are **hardly** any tickets left for the concert.

no, none, not, nothing   Do not use any of these negative words with another negative word.

NONSTANDARD	Yolanda asked for some correction fluid, but I don't have none.
STANDARD	Yolanda asked for some correction fluid, but I do**n't** have **any.**
NONSTANDARD	"I didn't do nothing," said the suspect.
STANDARD	"I did**n't** do **any**thing," said the suspect.

EXERCISE 6   Correcting Errors in Usage

In each of the following sentences, draw a line through the error in usage. Write the correct form above the error. [Note: There may be more than one way to correct each error.]

any

EX.   1.   There isn't ~~no~~ reason to be afraid.

or

is

     1.   There ~~isn't~~ no reason to be afraid.

1.   I couldn't barely hear my baby brother crying for his bottle.

2. Giorgio didn't have no papers on his desk during the exam.

3. I heard her say that she didn't do nothing wrong.

4. Doris doesn't have no more time to practice her trumpet.

5. We hadn't scarcely enough orange juice for the family at breakfast yesterday.

6. I looked for clues concerning his disappearance but didn't find nothing for several weeks.

7. "I don't want no more trouble," the frustrated shopkeeper exclaimed at the town meeting.

8. I haven't never seen no marsupials, even on television.

9. My grandmother Alba hasn't never left her beautiful homeland of Puerto Rico.

10. Soon-Yi doesn't have no easy answers to that complicated problem.

11. Do you think it's true that sailors never really saw nothing like a true mermaid?

12. I couldn't hardly complain about my convenient work schedule.

13. Diane wanted some popcorn, but we didn't have none in the pantry.

14. There aren't no more potatoes in the sack.

15. I don't know nothing about fixing clogged drains.

16. "I don't want no dessert," the diner said to the server.

17. Before last night, I hadn't never seen a shooting star.

18. I can't believe they still haven't done nothing about that leak.

19. Do not give no money to that phony organization.

20. Jasper wanted to sing campfire songs, but we didn't know none.

EXERCISE 7   Creating a Safety Poster

As a student in the food preparations program, you have been asked to create a poster of ten safety rules. On your own paper, write the ten rules that students should follow as they work. In at least five of the sentences, be sure you use a negative expression correctly.

EX.   1.   *Do not use the meat slicer without the blade guard in place.*

MODULE REVIEW

A. Identifying and Correcting Errors in Usage

In each of the following sentences, draw a line through the error in usage. Then write the correct usage in the space above the word. Some sentences may be correct.

                     affected

EX.   1. The drought ~~effected~~ this season's corn crops.

1. We reached a dead end and realized that this was all the farther we could go.

2. In my poem I made an illusion to the Iraq War.

3. The engraved invitation was to a party for the alumni of a girls' prep school.

4. Marta couldn't find her dance shoes anywheres.

5. Where did you find those South American instruments at?

6. The reason for the dress code is because company employees need to look presentable to customers.

7. Being that it was getting quite cold, we decided to move the party inside.

8. The soprano soloist sounded like she had a head cold.

9. You should of put air in the tires before putting them on the car.

10. What kind of a hockey stick are you using?

11. My brother he is learning to speak Swahili, an African language.

12. That kind of a dog makes an excellent playmate for children.

13. I want to study law just like my mother did.

14. You can get a hall pass off of the teacher.

15. Someone left a vase of flowers at the door, but neither María or I saw who did it.

16. Hanging art prints on the wall improved the appearance of the room some.

17. My grandmother immigrated from the Soviet Union in 1992.

18. This here colt comes from a long line of champion thoroughbreds.

19. Emilio enjoys horror films, but I have never liked that type of movie.

20. Panning is when you move the camera slowly from one side of a scene to another.

21. No one prepares Chinese food better than my father does.

22. Even though it was the first time Lee had skied downhill, he was kind of pleased.

23. The increases in enrollment effect the number of available dormitory rooms.

24. Six miles per hour is all the faster that this old car can go.

25. Have you finished folding that there laundry, Tom?

B.   Proofreading a Paragraph for Errors in Usage

In the paragraph below, draw a line through the errors in usage. Then write the correct usage in the space above the word. Some sentences may be correct.

EX.   [1] Sarah Winnemucca is an American Indian woman ~~which~~ *whom* we learned about in our history class.

[1] When she was young, there weren't hardly any European Americans in her part of Nevada. [2] Soon, however, white settlers arrived, and Sara's people, the Paiutes, were moved from their land onto a reservation. [3] Because the Paiutes, they were hungry on the reservation, they took some of the settlers' cattle. [4] This here action was unacceptable to the whites, who raided the Paiute camp. [5] Later, Sarah Winnemucca wrote a book about these experiences in which she was kind of blunt about broken agreements made between the U.S. government and the Paiute people.

C. Writing a Newspaper Article

You and some other students have just toured a factory that is making self-driving cars. Your science teacher has asked you to describe your experience for the school newspaper. On your own paper, write a brief article about self-driving cars. Include why you think they are or are not a good idea. In your article, use at least ten of the following expressions correctly.

affect	illusion	nowhere	kind of
effect	anyway	reason … is that	neither … nor
as far as	anywhere	could have	somewhat
as fast as	everywhere	than	type of

EX.   kind of
This kind of car may cause more accidents.

PEOPLE AND PLACES

12a   Capitalize the names of persons.

EXAMPLES   Ella Fitzgerald, Fred Rogers, Simone Biles

Some names contain more than one capital letter. Usage varies in the capitalization of *van, von, du, de la,* and other parts of many multiword names. Always verify the spelling of a name with the person, or check the name in a reference source.

EXAMPLES   La Fontaine   McEwen   O'Conner   Van Doren
            Yellow Thunder   Ibn Ezra   Villa-Lobos   van Gogh

12b   Capitalize geographical names.

Type of Name	Examples
towns, cities	Madison, Augusta, Topeka, Springfield
counties, states	Litchfield County, Wayne County, Alaska, Idaho
countries	Australia, Portugal, Romania, Peru, Mali
islands	Java, Madagascar, Tasmania, Iceland, Florida Keys
bodies of water	Pacific Ocean, Bay of Bengal, Lake Superior
forests, parks	Bryce Canyon National Park, Constitution Gardens
streets, highways	New Jersey Turnpike, Route 128, Interstate 93
mountains	Himalayas, Rocky Mountains, Andes
continents	Africa, South America, Europe, Asia
regions	the South, the Midwest

NOTE   Words such as *east, west, north*, and *south* are not capitalized when they indicate direction.
  EXAMPLES   I traveled north for one hour.
      Joni lives west of the school.

NOTE   In a hyphenated street number, the second part of the number is not capitalized.
  EXAMPLE   East Seventy-eighth Street

EXERCISE 1   Correcting Errors in Capitalization

For each sentence below, correct the errors in capitalization by drawing a line through each incorrect word. Write your corrections on the line before each sentence.

EX.   _Sleepytime Drive_   1.   We moved to ~~sleepytime drive~~.

_____   1. My sister found the indian ocean on the map.

_____   2. Have you dreamed of climbing mount everest, which is located on the eastern border of nepal?

_____   3. Who was the first European to see the amazon river?

_____   4. The caspian sea is fed by eight different rivers.

_____   5. The aguilar family wants to visit the cayman islands, which are 150 miles South of cuba.

_____   6. My class went to the kenai fjords national park.

_____   7. Our friend pascal enjoyed his visit to albany, New York.

_____   8. The principal, fran washington, worked at a school in the midwest last year.

_____   9. Travel north on route 1 to essex county.

_____   10. "How long is the missouri river?" Ty asked.

EXERCISE 2   Proofreading Sentences for Correct Capitalization

In the sentences below, underline the words that should be capitalized, and write the corrections above the words. Some sentences may be correct.

Interstate
EX.   1.   Repairs are being made on interstate 84.

1. I would like to visit lake tahoe in california.

2. I think boston, the capital of massachusetts, is a beautiful city.

3. Whenever I travel to the south, I visit cypress gardens, florida.

4. My older sister gertie lives at west fifty-sixth street.

5. I enjoy the view of the adirondack mountains from lake george.

6. The group traveled north along the eastern slope.

7. The danube river travels through the major cities of eastern europe.

8. Kings's Canyon national park is in the sierra nevada range.

9. Is Australia a Continent or an Island, or is it both?

10. To get to buffalo, new york, from syracuse, take the new york state thruway, or interstate 90, west.

MODULE 12: CAPITAL LETTERS

SCHOOL SUBJECTS, FIRST WORDS, PROPER ADJECTIVES

12c Do *not* capitalize the names of school subjects, except for names of languages and course names followed by a number.

EXAMPLES   art   chemistry   algebra   music

                 Spanish   English   Geometry I   History II

12d Capitalize the first word in every sentence.

EXAMPLES   **I** crocheted a sweater. **It** was a gift for Lee.

The first word of a sentence that is a direct quotation is capitalized even if the quotation begins within a sentence.

EXAMPLE   Dora said, "**My** aloe plant is on the windowsill."

Traditionally, the first word in a line of poetry is capitalized.

EXAMPLES   **S**unflowers filled the ragged front yard

                 And faced the street, as if to stand guard.

The pronoun *I* and the interjection *O* are capitalized whether or not they are the first words of sentences. The common interjection *oh* is capitalized only when it begins a sentence or is part of a title.

EXAMPLES   **I** replaced the flat tire; then **I** got back on the freeway.

                 Sherry titled her essay "**O** the Way West: **Oh** the Things We Saw."

12e Capitalize proper nouns and proper adjectives.

A *common noun* names any one of a group of people, places, or things. A *proper noun* names a particular person, place, or thing. A *proper adjective* is formed from a proper noun.

Proper Nouns	Proper Adjectives
Brazil	Brazilian dance
Queen Victoria	Victorian house
Irish	Irish literature

NOTE   Proper nouns and proper adjectives may lose their capitals after long use.

        EXAMPLES   sandwich   china   diesel

EXERCISE 3   Using Capital Letters Correctly

For each sentence below, correct the errors in capitalization by drawing a line through each error and writing the correct form in the space above it.

EX.   1.   Adrian said, "~~my~~ *M* shoes are wet."

1. I think my latin class will help me in my future studies.

2. Since we moved, we often miss the beautiful hawaiian weather.

3. Marcus and Lydia are going to wait until the spring of the next school year to take algebra II, i heard.

4. One of Rodney's most interesting poems begins with the line, "rain fell on the roof."

5. Cousin Elena made delicious spanish rice for the town banquet.

6. how long did it take you to learn the art of making paper?

7. Katrina received a long letter from her japanese pen pal yesterday.

8. Sadly, my grandmother lost some antique China during that earthquake.

9. My uncle said, "the cat and the dog need fresh water and food before we leave."

10. We were all wondering if Leonardo's new italian restaurant attracted a lot of business.

11. In Art class, Rita made earrings with colorful wooden beads and copper wires, and oh, are they lovely!

12. I was moved by the poem that opened with the line, "the child's smile lit up her grandfather's face."

13. The mayor said, "o city! you should be proud!"

14. I've heard that history III focuses on the twentieth century.

15. Ed told them that ethiopian food is available on Tremont Street.

16. We read wonderful short stories in my english class this year.

17. I would like to interview our property owner. she is armenian.

18. Mariah said, "my favorite color is purple."

19. do you understand why i had to do that?

20. I love my father's french onion soup.

GROUPS, ORGANIZATIONS, AND RELIGIONS

12f Capitalize the names of teams, organizations, businesses, institutions, buildings, and government bodies

Type of Name	Examples
teams	Montreal Canadiens, Indiana Pacers, New York Giants
organizations	Wilderness Society American Heart Association
businesses	Family Car Care Dragon Light Restaurant
institutions	Louisiana State University, Lahey Clinic
buildings	Rialto Theater, Sears Tower
government bodies	Internal Revenue Service, U.S. Air Force, U.S. Postal Service

NOTE   The names of organizations, businesses, and government bodies are often abbreviated as a series of capital letters.

EXAMPLES   Federal Bureau of Investigation   **FBI**

Environmental Protection Agency   **EPA**

Commission on Civil Rights   **CCR**

12g Capitalize the names of specific nationalities and peoples.

EXAMPLES   Asian, Hispanic, African American, Caucasian, Inuit, Chinese, Italian, Polish

12h Capitalize the names of religions and their followers, holy days, sacred writings, and specific deities.

EXAMPLES   Taoism, Judaism, Easter, Ramadan, Old Testament, Koran, Torah, God, Allah, Buddha

EXERCISE 4   Identifying Correct Capitalization

Write the letter *C* on the line before each phrase that is capitalized correctly.

EX. _____   1.   a.   north shore linen service

__*C*__   b.   North Shore Linen Service

_____   1.   a.   the Chinese   _____   6.   a.   Scott's Auto clinic

_____   b.   the chinese   _____   b.   Scott's Auto Clinic

_____   2.   a.   Endicott college   _____   7.   a.   Children's Hospital

_____   b.   Endicott College   _____   b.   a Children's Doctor

_____   3.   a.   a Seattle Fishery   _____   8.   a.   c. i. a.

_____   b.   Seattle Mariners   _____   b.   CIA

_____   4.   a.   National Guard   _____   9.   a.   the holy spirit

_____   b.   National Defense   _____   b.   the Holy Spirit

_____   5.   a.   hinduism   _____   10.   a.   the russians

_____   b.   Hinduism   _____   b.   the Russians

EXERCISE 5   Proofreading Sentences for Correct Capitalization

For each sentence below, correct the errors in capitalization by drawing a line through each error and writing the correct form above it. Some sentences may contain no errors.

EX.   1.   Most participants in shintoism are asian.
                              S   *A*

1.   I think the coast guard has issued a warning.

2.   My father has worked at giovanni's barbershop for eleven years.

3.   On christmas Pastor Reeves read several passages from the new testament.

4.   Meredith read about the royal astronomical society of canada.

5.   We ate a good breakfast of English muffins and fresh fruit before going to the new england patriots game.

6.   The U.S. department of health and human services sent a memo.

7.   They towed the car to tony's house of tires.

8.   Dana volunteers at Yale-new haven hospital every week.

9.   We will celebrate the jewish holiday yom kippur.

10.   I would like to work in the theater.

OBJECTS, EVENTS, AND AWARDS

12i   **Capitalize the brand names of business products.**

EXAMPLES   **B**orden milk, **B**ridgestone tires, **N**eutrogena soap

12j   **Capitalize the names of historical events and periods, special events, and calendar items.**

EXAMPLES   **C**ivil **W**ar, **M**iddle **A**ges, **O**lympics, **N**ew **Y**ear's **D**ay, **C**hing **M**ing **F**estival, **F**riday, **J**une

12k   **Capitalize the names of ships, monuments, awards, planets, and any other particular places, things, or events.**

Type of Name	Examples
ships, trains	USS *Nautilus*, Express Metroliner
aircraft, spacecraft, missiles	Lockheed, *Atlantis*, *Apollo 11*
monuments, memorials	Fort Frederica, Statue of Liberty
awards	Caldecott Medal, Tony Awards
planets, stars, constellations	Neptune, Sirius, Ursa Major

EXERCISE 6   Proofreading Sentences for Correct Capitalization

For each sentence below, correct the errors in capitalization by drawing a line though the incorrect word. Write your corrections on the line before each sentence. If a sentence is correct, write *C*.

EX.   _____*Venus*_____   1. Cam saw the planet ~~venus~~ through a telescope.

_____   1. The united states marine corps war memorial in Washington, D.C., is also known as *Iwo Jima*.

_____   2. The tanker *grand zenith* sank off Cape Cod, Massachusetts, January 11, 1977.

_____   3. St. lucia's day is a late-december celebration worth attending.

_____   4. My report on the louisiana purchase is due next wednesday.

_____   5. I had coupons for progresso bread crumbs and meow mix cat food.

_____   6. My grandfather received one medal, a purple heart, because he was injured in the line of duty.

_____ 7. Can you see the north star or the big dipper?

_____ 8. "I will be describing the cenozoic era in history," the teacher said.

_____ 9. My mother, a respected poet, has won a guggenheim fellowship.

_____ 10. Jethro saw photographs of the plane *graf zeppelin.*

_____ 11. Miles would love to win a "young artist auditions" scholarship.

_____ 12. That book explains the spanish-american war.

_____ 13. Can Rafael distinguish a boeing 747 from other types of planes?

_____ 14. That space museum has a display on project apollo, the space program.

_____ 15. Jacob and I think saturn must be the most interesting planet to see.

_____ 16. During the ice age, large portions of the earth were covered with ice.

_____ 17. On monday we will watch a long filmstrip about *sputnik II.*

_____ 18. Will the olympics this winter feature figure skating?

_____ 19. If you study the harlem renaissance, you will surely read about the writer Zora Neale Hurston.

_____ 20. The star you saw saturday night may have been betelgeuse.

_____ 21. Arlo Guthrie wrote a song about a train ride on the *city of New Orleans.*

_____ 22. One of the few constellations I recognize is orion.

_____ 23. My stepbrother is a fighter jet test pilot in France.

_____ 24. Pablo's lifelong dream was to win the national book award.

_____ 25. If I never travel to mars, I won't be surprised.

MODULE 12: CAPITAL LETTERS
TITLES

12l   Capitalize titles.

(1) Capitalize the title of a person when the title comes before the name.

EXAMPLES   My doctor, **D**r. Rivera, was on call last night.
I saw **G**overnor Weicker at the event.

(2) Capitalize a word showing a family relationship when the word is used before or in place of a person's name but not when preceded by a possessive.

EXAMPLES   We prepared dinner for **D**ad and **U**ncle Oscar.
Has my **a**unt Millie met your **g**randmother?

(3) Capitalize the first and last words and all important words in titles of books, newspapers, magazines, poems, short stories, historical documents, movies, television programs, and works of art and music.

Unimportant words in titles include articles (*a, an, the*), coordinating conjunctions (*and, but, for, nor, or, so, yet*), or prepositions of fewer than five letters (*at, for, from, with*).

NOTE   An article (*a, an,* or *the*) before a title is not capitalized unless it is the first word of the title.

Type of Title	Examples
books	*Walden,* **Because** of ***Winn-Dixie***
newspapers	*Baltimore Sun, Detroit News*
magazines	*Discover, Backpacker, Essence*
poems	"**A** Blessing", "**T**he **R**ed **W**heelbarrow"
short stories	"Mana Seda", "Split Cherry Tree"
historical documents	the **M**agna **C**arta
movies	*The Hunger Games, Jurassic* **World**
television programs	*The Simpsons, The Voice*
works of art	*Autumn Rhythm, Pieta*
works of music	*We Can't Dance, Peer Gynt Suite*

EXERCISE 7   Proofreading for Correct Capitalization

For each sentence below, correct the errors in capitalization by drawing a line through the error and writing the correct form in the space above it. Some sentences may be correct.

                 S

EX.   1.   Hoping to become ~~senator~~ Ferraro, Geraldine Anne Ferraro ran against Alfonse D'Amato of New York.

1. Our science teacher read to us a passage from Edward O. Wilson's book *the diversity of life.*

2. Lois Rosenthal edited a magazine called *story.*

3. Did your Sister Susan write a thank-you note to uncle Emilio?

4. Have you read "aardvark," Julia Fields' poem about Malcolm X?

5. Maika says that the *oakland post* is her favorite newspaper.

6. Between 2007 and 2019, The Big Bang Theory was one of the most popular shows on television.

7. The best-selling nonfiction book in 2016 was Paul Kalanithi's *when breath becomes air.*

8. You need to make an appointment to see the doctor.

9. Was the longest-running television program in history *the wonderful world of disney*?

10. I love Auguste Rodin's sculpture *the thinker.*

11. Lincoln issued the emancipation proclamation on January 1, 1863.

12. I thought the movie *guardians of the galaxy* was quite funny.

13. In school we read the book *ragtime* by E. L. Doctorow.

14. My neighbor, professor Rivera, teaches Mexican history.

15. The *tacoma morning news tribune* is published in Washington state.

16. In 1783, the treaty of paris ended the American Revolution.

17. Will aunt Dolores be traveling to Paraguay again this year?

18. Haruki Murakami wrote the story "the little green monster."

19. I have long admired the Nez Perce leader chief Joseph.

20. Didn't Vincent van Gogh paint that wonderful work called *the starry night?*

MODULE REVIEW

A. Correcting Errors in Capitalization

For each sentence below, correct the errors in capitalization by drawing a line through the error and writing the correct form in the space above it.

EX. 1. Mom's best friend, ~~dr. r~~utkowski, teaches at a junior college. *(D R)*

1. "have you ever seen a cincinnati team play?" asked Rolf.

2. sally and matt ate at a thai restaurant called bow thai.

3. The offices of the united nations children's fund are located at three un plaza, new york, new york.

4. Do you really think that Uncle Maxwell once worked for the cia?

5. We saw mary cassatt's painting *the boating party* at the national gallery of art in washington, d. c.

6. aunt harriet is writing a book called *how to be a kid till the day you die.*

7. I wanted to buy some of Jackson's piccadilly brand herbal tea, so I went to cape ann market on eastern avenue.

8. on valentine's day we visted the petrified forest national park in arizona; then we returned home on a southwest airlines flight.

9. Chandra looked for a copy of Helene Chirinian's book *camping out* at the chicago public library.

10. My brother showed me a poem called "choices," written by nikki giovanni; he had read it in an english class at gordon college.

B. Proofreading for Correct Capitalization

On your own paper, correct the capitalization errors in the paragraph below. Some sentences may be correct.

EX. [1] Two large islands, north island and south island, make up most of the country of new zealand.

[1] *North Island; South Island; New Zealand*

[1] We were told this and many other interesting facts about new zealand history and geography by dr. Flo Marino. [2] She gave a lecture at the downtown library yesterday. [3] Dr. marino teaches cartography at the university but spends all of her free time in the south pacific. [4] Besides the two main islands, the country includes stewart island and several other small islands. [5] Large cities in new zealand include auckland, manukau, wellington, and christchurch. [6] Located in the south on the tasman sea is fiordland national park. [7] Through this park runs part of the mountain range known as the southern alps. [8] New Zealand has many rivers, including the waikato river in the north and the clutha river in the south. [9] The islands were first settled by a polynesian people known as the maoris. [10] Dr. marino said that her frequent trips to New Zealand give her the opportunity to explore her maori heritage.

C. Writing a Letter

You've just started writing to a teenager in India. You and your pen pal are eager to learn more about each other's cultures. Write a letter of at least ten sentences to your pen pal. Describe some custom or practice that is unique to United States culture or special to your family. In your letter, apply five of the rules of capitalization given in this module.

EX. *April 3, 2020*

Dear Amit,

How are things in Bombay? I really enjoyed your last letter, especially the part about the trip that you took with your family to Varanasi on the Ganges River.

My family has never made a pilgrimage, but we do have special celebrations and traditions. Perhaps you have heard of Thanksgiving Day? On this day in November, we try to remember and to be grateful for all the good things in our lives. Thanksgiving Day celebrates a time in early American history when American Indians helped the English colonists and then shared with them a special meal. So, on Thanksgiving, we eat special meals and remember that time in our history.

Write again soon,
Emily

End marks—periods, question marks, exclamation points—are used to indicate the purpose of a sentence.

13a   A statement (or declarative sentence) ends with a period.

EXAMPLES   Yoshi is feeding the dog.
                Elaine went to the market.

13b   A question (or interrogative sentence) ends with a question mark.

EXAMPLES   Have you washed the dishes yet?
                Who was that boy I saw you talking to?

(1) Do not use a question mark after a declarative sentence stating an indirect question.

DECLARATIVE   Stevie wondered who would win.
INTERROGATIVE   Do you think you will win?

(2) Commands and requests are often put in question form even when they aren't actually questions. In that case, they may be followed by either a period or a question mark.

EXAMPLES   Will you please state your name.
                Will you please state your name?

(3) Place a question mark inside the closing quotation marks when the quotation itself is a question. Otherwise, place a question mark outside the closing quotation marks.

EXAMPLES   He asked, "Where is my smartphone?"
                Did you say "smartphone"?

13c   An exclamation ends with an exclamation point.

EXAMPLES   How disgusting!   I don't believe it!   Hey!

Place an exclamation point inside the closing quotation marks when the quotation itself is an exclamation. Otherwise, place the exclamation point outside the quotation marks.

EXAMPLES   At the graduation exercises the class cheered, "Yea, Carlos!"
                I thought you said "Time's up"!

13d   An imperative sentence may end with either a period or an exclamation point.

EXAMPLES   Please hand me that wrench. [request]
             Give me that! [a command]

Sometimes a command is stated in question form. However, since its purpose is to give a command or make a request, it may be followed by a period or an exclamation point.

EXAMPLES   Will you get off my foot!   May we get through, please.

EXERCISE 1   Correcting Sentences by Adding End Marks

Add the proper end mark to each of the following items. Some items may have more than one correct answer.

EX.   1. Are we going now?

1. Where are you
2. Walter renewed his driver's license
3. Stop right now
4. Running barefoot through the grass can be fun
5. Do students go to school during Ramadan
6. What an incredible film
7. Don't say a word
8. Where I come from, cricket is a very popular sport
9. Go, Patriots, go
10. Why do you think so
11. Believe it or not, Sergio wrote me a letter
12. Please don't go out after dark
13. Move over there
14. We knew she was already here
15. Watch out
16. Tell me if everyone has accepted the invitation
17. Have you ever been to the *Carnaval* parade in Veracruz
18. Are you kidding
19. A magnet attracts metal
20. How are the driving conditions today

ABBREVIATIONS

13e   **An abbreviation is usually followed by a period.**

Abbreviations with Periods	
Personal Names Titles Used with Names States	Diane T. Wilson, W. C. Fields Dr., Jr., Sr., Mr., Mrs., Ms. N.Mex., Ga., Conn., Wash.
Organizations and Companies	Co., Inc., Corp., Assn.
Addresses	St., Rd., Ave., P.O. Box, Blvd.
Times	A.M., P.M., A.D., B.C.
Abbreviations without Periods	
Government Agencies	FBI, CIA, FDA, NASA
State Abbreviations Followed by ZIP Code	Jackson, AL 36545 Willows, CA 95988
Units of Measure	cm, kg, ml, oz, ft, yd, mi, lb
Widely Used Abbreviations	DVD, PTA, NAACP, UNICEF, TV

NOTE   Two-letter state codes are used only when the ZIP Code is included. These state codes are not followed by periods.

       EXAMPLE   Springfield, **MA** 01101

NOTE   In most cases, an abbreviation is capitalized only if the words that it stands for are capitalized. If you are unsure whether to use periods with an abbreviation or whether to capitalize it, check a dictionary.

EXERCISE 2   Proofreading for Correct Punctuation of Abbreviations

In the items below, add or delete any periods where needed. Some items may be correct.

    EX.   1.   Dr. Jane R. Otis

1. 1-hr. service
2. NFL
3. Dr. Ana P Carr
4. 50 m.m.

5. Concord, NH 03301
6. Freeyklund Construction Co
7. Orlando, Fla

8. 12 ½ Davis St
9. 3:00 P M sharp
10. 50-yd. dash

REVIEW EXERCISE

A.   Proofreading Sentences for Correct Punctuation

In the sentences below, add punctuation where needed. Some sentences may be correct.

EX.   1.   I hear Constance caught a 6-in fish

1.   When did Roberto leave for the Main St station

2.   We thought it unusual that he signed his name D T R Parker

3.   Was it really 10:00 A M before they arrived

4.   Don't debate about the Panama Canal

5.   Sometimes the newscasters on CBS, NBC, and ABC refer to former presidents as FDR, JFK, and LBJ.

6.   I can't believe he actually ran 50 ft. that fast

7.   The letter was addressed to Dr Manuel T Clemente

8.   What famous person was born at 5:00 P M in 40 B C

9.   They mailed the 4-lb. package to a P O Box in Honolulu

10.   Pitcairn Island in the South Pacific measures 1.5 sq mi

13f   Use commas to separate items in a series.

WORDS   I am going to the riverside cleanup day with Marcie, Latrice, Betty, and Dominic.

PHRASES   We looked for the glasses in my bedroom, in the car, in my hall locker, and in my gym locker.

CLAUSES   Mr. Hartry said that we had worked hard, that we had improved immensely, and that we would put on a terrific show.

NOTE   Some paired words—such as *macaroni and cheese* or *shoes and socks*—may be considered a single item.

EXAMPLE   Shimon put on his pants, shoes and socks, and jacket.

13g   **If all items in a series are joined by *and, or*, or *nor*, do not separate them with commas.**

EXAMPLES   Washington **and** Oregon **and** Idaho are three states I'd like to visit next summer.

Do you swim in the upper pond **or** the lower pond **or** the creek?

13h   **Use commas to separate two or more adjectives preceding a noun.**

EXAMPLES   Marge had a wonderful, happy, exciting day with her uncle. Ulna is an imaginative, expressive, determined artist.

EXERCISE 3   Proofreading Sentences for the Correct Use of Commas

In the following sentences, insert commas where needed. Draw a line through any unnecessary commas. If the sentence is correct, write *C* on the line before the sentence.

EX. _____ 1. Bring forks, knives, spoons, and napkins/to the picnic.

_____   1. Joachim won the talent show by singing well being polite and dressing appropriately.

_____   2. By the end of the game, the basket seemed two inches around one thousand yards away and ten miles high.

_____   3. These hats come in black, and green, and brown.

_____   4. Red blue and yellow are the primary colors.

_____   5. His favorite foods are potatoes, corn and peas.

_____ 6. My sister enjoys all the holidays: Christmas Easter Thanksgiving and Valentine's Day.

_____ 7. Ricardo and Bill and Consuela and Sam were elected class officers.

_____ 8. "What a marvelous wonderful terrific incredible day!" she enthusiastically exclaimed.

_____ 9. Who doesn't know about Happy Dopey Grumpy Sleepy Doc and the rest of the dwarves?

_____ 10. Lunch consisted of both ham and cheese and peanut butter and jelly sandwiches.

_____ 11. Neither rain, nor snow, nor dark of night stopped the fearless explorers.

_____ 12. Thanks for the flowers and candy for the kind words and for everything else you did during that long week.

_____ 13. Pick any direction: north or south or east or west.

_____ 14. Nobody knew who the burglars were when exactly they had broken in what they took or where they went.

_____ 15. Thank you good luck and goodnight.

_____ 16. It's Halloween, but I'm not sure if we're going trick-or-treating.

_____ 17. Visiting the Washington Monument the Jefferson Memorial and the White House was a remarkable experience.

_____ 18. Domingo was amazed that he wasn't winded grateful that his feet didn't hurt and delighted that he'd won.

_____ 19. You can get a ticket by going over the speed limit double-parking failing to use the turn signal or driving without proper registration.

_____ 20. Rudolph was finally accepted by Donner Blixen Comet and Cupid.

_____ 21. These musicals were written by the well-known teams of Rodgers and Hammerstein and Lerner and Loewe.

_____ 22. Go over the hill cross the plain walk through those pines find the cave and you'll see the underground waterfall.

_____ 23. Neither Lulu nor Susan nor Bianca could stand to wear the turquoise sweater.

_____ 24. Hopeful cautious and ready, we waited.

_____ 25. The last ones to rent scuba gear were Marie Che Marge and Don.

COMMAS WITH INDEPENDENT CLAUSES

13i **Use commas before *and, but, for, nor, or, so,* and *yet* when they join independent clauses.**

EXAMPLE   Morgan threw the baseball hard, and Hu caught it.

NOTE   Before *for, so,* and *yet* joining independent clauses, always use a comma. However, before *and, but, nor,* and *or,* the comma may be omitted if (1) the clauses are very short and (2) there is no possibility of misunderstanding either clause.

    CORRECT   I talked **but** nobody listened.

    INCORRECT   I talked to Sam and Jens and Rita danced.

    CORRECT   I talked to Sam, and Jens and Rita danced.

Do not confuse a compound sentence with a simple sentence that has a compound verb.

    SIMPLE SENTENCE   I folded my clothes **and** put them away. [one independent clause with a compound verb]

    COMPOUND SENTENCE   I folded my clothes, and I put them away. [two independent clauses]

13j **Independent clauses in a series are usually separated by semicolons. Short independent clauses, however, may be separated by commas.**

EXAMPLES   On our vacation we drove through the woods; we hiked up a mountain; and we swam in the Pacific Ocean.
On our vacation we drove, we hiked, and we swam.

EXERCISE 4   Correcting Punctuation in Sentences

For each of the following sentences, insert commas where needed. If a sentence is correct, write *C* on the line before the sentence.

    EX.   _____   1. Flags are used to represent nations, but they are also used to send messages.

_____   1. Flags may be placed in various arrangements on a line or they can be held by a signaler, using a method known as semaphore.

_____   2. Semaphore was invented in the late 1700s and it was widely used until the arrival of the telegraph.

_____   3. The distance between the semaphore posts still is often great and the signalers use telescopes to read each other's messages.

_____ 4. Each signaler holds two flags, one in the left hand and one in the right.

_____ 5. The signalers send messages over water and they use red and yellow flags; but over land the signal colors are red and white.

_____ 6. One can read a message from the pattern of the flags and send an answer back right away.

_____ 7. Some flag positions represent letters but others stand for numbers.

_____ 8. People used semaphore less after the 1830s for about that time Samuel Morse invented the electric telegraph.

_____ 9. Morse developed the telegraph and created a code to go with it.

_____ 10. Various patterns of dots and dashes represent numbers and letters.

_____ 11. These dots and dashes don't correspond to the colors or positions of flags; but with this code signalers can send messages much farther.

_____ 12. Telegraphy is a more efficient way to send messages yet even it has disadvantages.

_____ 13. During a sea battle two friendly ships may be able to trade messages rapidly but the radio signals might also give away their position to the enemy.

_____ 14. "Be silent or be sunk" might be the rule in some situations.

_____ 15. The code may be sophisticated but it still can be intercepted.

_____ 16. Morse code and similar systems are now the standard everywhere for the old-fashioned way of using flags to send messages has been replaced for the most part.

_____ 17. The international flag code consists of twenty-six flags and each flag stands for a different letter of the alphabet.

_____ 18. The sailors on ships may not be able to speak one another's languages but they can still communicate using the flag code.

_____ 19. Single flags can sometimes stand for an entire message so the letter "V" may mean "I need assistance."

_____ 20. Ship flags can carry coded messages or they can be national flags that identify the ship's native country.

_____ 21. On merchant ships, flags can be national flags or merchant flags.

_____ 22. National flags usually show one or more of the following colors: yellow, green, white, black, blue, red, and orange.

_____ 23. Flags of ships from Muslim countries often have a crescent and star and many flags from Christian countries have crosses on them.

_____ 24. On Britain's flag, the red cross stands for England the white cross stands for Scotland and the blue field stands for Ireland.

_____ 25. The national flag of the United States also uses red white and blue; but the stripes represent the original thirteen states and the stars represent the modern fifty states.

COMMAS WITH NONESSENTIAL ELEMENTS

13k Use commas to set off nonessential participial phrases and nonessential clauses.

EXAMPLES   The woman, exhausted by the heat, took a drink of water.
My new stepfather, who works in a bank, is named Edward.

A *nonessential* (or *nonrestrictive*) phrase or clause is one containing information that is not needed to understand the main idea of the sentence.

NONESSENTIAL PHRASE   The critic, pleased with our performance, wrote a good review of our show.

NONESSENTIAL CLAUSE   Our class party, which we have been planning, will take place this Saturday afternoon.

An *essential* (or *restrictive*) clause or phrase is one that cannot be omitted without changing the meaning of the sentence.

ESSENTIAL PHRASE   The man **carrying the luggage** was walking slowly.

ESSENTIAL CLAUSE   The team **that fills the most garbage bags** will win a trip to Mount Rushmore.

NOTE   Adjective clauses beginning with *that*, like the one in the last example above, are nearly always essential.

EXERCISE 5   Correcting Sentences by Adding Commas

For each of the following sentences, identify the italicized phrase or clause by writing *e.* for *essential* or *n.e.* for *nonessential* on the line before the sentence. Insert commas where needed.

EX. _*n.e.*_   1. Our uncle Ben, *who played for the Phillies* came for the holidays.

_____   1. We picked up Cousin Mathilda at the exact time *that she had requested in her text*.

_____   2. Rodrigo *skeptical of airplanes* always took the train.

_____   3. Ali *having worked for the city of Tucson for thirty years* had just retired.

_____   4. The tour group watched as the three seals *no longer interested in watching the people from the rocks* plunged back into the water.

_____   5. Carl *proud of his accomplishment* bragged a little.

_____   6. He was one of those rolling stones *that gathers no moss*.

_____ 7. Nobody *who met Dixie* could help liking her.

_____ 8. Send the forty pounds of paper to that manufacturer *who will recycle it.*

_____ 9. The students *excited by the arrival of the guest speaker* filed into the auditorium.

_____ 10. The actors *enjoying the moment* smiled and bowed to the audience.

_____ 11. The jockey *who had crossed the finish line first* received the trophy.

_____ 12. Anoki's store *which features original handmade prints* opened yesterday.

_____ 13. The agent *unnoticed by the crowd* quietly left the room.

_____ 14. Kim *who brought the tomatoes* sat down to make the salad.

_____ 15. I don't know what I'd do without that clock *which helps me to be on time.*

_____ 16. The children *hoping to see their favorite clown again* returned to the circus.

_____ 17. Ring the bell *that has the name "Martinez" printed next to it.*

_____ 18. Mrs. Thompson *noticing the students' restlessness* dismissed the class early.

_____ 19. Do you know *who did it*?

_____ 20. There were rumors that Mr. Cleburne *whom we all knew to live on North Street* had recently moved.

_____ 21. Only the soldiers *carrying the equipment* were allowed to rest.

_____ 22. Tell Max *which one to take.*

_____ 23. The store was advertising that new brand of soap *which nobody had tried yet.*

_____ 24. The skier *racing down the hill recklessly* almost hit a tree.

_____ 25. Emilio was determined to learn how to play tennis, a sport *that had always interested him.*

COMMAS WITH INTRODUCTORY ELEMENTS

13l   **Use a comma after certain introductory elements.**

(1)   **Use a comma after interjections such as** *hey, oh, well,* **and** *why,* **and after other introductory words such as** *yes* **and** *no.*

EXAMPLES   **Well,** this is rather surprising.
                 Hey, what are you doing here?
                 No, thank you, I do not want more rice now.

(2)   **Use a comma after an introductory participial phrase.**

EXAMPLES   **Turning to me,** she asked where the dining hall was.
                 Covered with rust, the antique trunk refused to open.

(3)   **Use a comma after two or more introductory prepositional phrases.**

EXAMPLES   **At the beginning of the day,** I feel energetic.
                 In the top drawer of the dresser near the door, you'll find the key.

(4)   **Use a comma after an introductory adverb clause.**

An introductory adverb clause may appear at the beginning of a sentence or before any independent clause in the sentence.

EXAMPLES   **If we leave now,** we won't be late.
                 I told Lin that I cannot work on the yearbook anymore; yet**, whenever he sees me,** he asks me to work on it.

EXERCISE 6   Correcting Sentences by Adding Commas

For each of the following sentences, insert commas where needed. If a sentence is correct, write *C* on the line before the sentence.

EX. _____ 1. In the cool of the morning, we walked to the shore.

_____   1.   Please I need to use the telephone.

_____   2.   Getting right to the point the coach drew a line across the center of the board.

_____   3.   Until you came along I didn't think anyone could do it.

_____   4.   In a pleasant valley across the snowcapped mountains they finally found water.

_____ 5. You may be leaving now; but wherever you go I'll be sure to write to you.

_____ 6. Yes they'll be back in an hour.

_____ 7. Singing the same old song, they sauntered slowly across the sand.

_____ 8. Until the break of day not a sound was heard in the cabin.

_____ 9. Reliable as ever the pilot steered the ship through the storm.

_____ 10. Decked out in several layers of clothing my cousins attended the New Year's Day parade.

_____ 11. No I don't want you to do that!

_____ 12. Curious as to what had made the noise Rachel opened the door.

_____ 13. They waited until everyone had left; and, before the moon rose, they made their escape.

_____ 14. Wait nobody move!

_____ 15. Having said what he needed to say Cornelius stopped talking.

_____ 16. Up the stairs to the right, there's a closet.

_____ 17. Thanking the two boys she left.

_____ 18. No matter how much you want to go you should think it over first.

_____ 19. Boy it's hot!

_____ 20. Almost more quickly than the eye could see the deer sprang across the road.

_____ 21. Maybe but let's vote on it.

_____ 22. Sticking the insect repellent in her pack Bea headed up the trail.

_____ 23. David said, "Well I guess I should have looked first!"

_____ 24. In the middle of the night, we watched the lunar eclipse.

_____ 25. When he answered the phone he was still half asleep.

MODULE 13: PUNCTUATION

COMMAS WITH SENTENCE INTERRUPTERS

13m   **Use commas to set off elements that interrupt the sentence.**

(1)   **Commas are usually used to set off appositives and appositive phrases.**

An *appositive* is a noun or pronoun that follows another noun or pronoun to identify or explain it. An *appositive phrase* consists of an appositive and its modifiers.

EXAMPLES   Team sports, **especially soccer,** are quite popular.
                 Julio, **the boy in the first row,** works for a repair shop.

Sometimes an appositive is so closely related to the word preceding it that it should not be set off by commas. Such an appositive is called a *restrictive appositive.*

EXAMPLES   My friend **Gar** helped me.
                 The publisher **Penguin Random House** produces paperback books.

(2)   **Use commas to set off words used in direct address.**

EXAMPLES   **Dad,** have you seen my toast?
                 Your briefcase, **Stella,** is in the rack by the door.
                 You played that ballad very well, **Rodney.**

(3)   **Use commas to set off parenthetical expressions.**

Parenthetical expressions are remarks that add incidental information or relate ideas to each other.

Commonly Used Parenthetical Expressions		
after all	I believe (hope, etc.)	naturally
at any rate	incidentally	nevertheless
by the way	in fact	of course
consequently	in general	on the contrary
for example	in the first place	on the other hand
for instance	meanwhile	that is
however	moreover	therefore

EXAMPLES   **On the contrary,** I have done it many times.
                 My whole-grain bread is, **in fact,** quite delicious.
                 I made two of those goals, **I believe.**

NOTE	A contrasting expression introduced by *not* or *yet* is parenthetical and must be set off by commas.
	EXAMPLES It was Franklin Roosevelt, **not Theodore,** who met Stalin and Churchill at Yalta.
	Hockey is similar to, **yet slightly different from,** lacrosse.

EXERCISE 7   Proofreading Sentences for Correct Use of Commas

For each of the sentences below, insert commas where needed. If a sentence is correct, write *C* on the line before the sentence.

EX. _____ 1. By the way, have you seen my camera?

_____ 1. My sister Phoebe got me to join the camera club.

_____ 2. She said, "Rick you need a hobby."

_____ 3. Consequently I joined the group.

_____ 4. My first camera though fairly inexpensive took fairly good pictures.

_____ 5. I still have the photograph I took of my cousin's horse Florence.

_____ 6. Of course the background of the picture is a little dark.

_____ 7. On the other hand I was just a beginner.

_____ 8. Naturally after a while I got a new camera one that made better pictures.

_____ 9. The camera club meets every Thursday afternoon at the home of Vicky Morales the club president.

_____ 10. Most of the time the meetings are informal not businesslike.

_____ 11. Nevertheless Rob Samuelson the club secretary occasionally takes notes for us.

_____ 12. Last month a debate began between Phoebe and Warner Hopkins an ace photographer.

_____ 13. Incidentally the discussion was over having a photo contest.

_____ 14. Phoebe said, "You just want to have a contest Warner because you know you'll win."

_____ 15. In fact we had the contest; and Phoebe my surprised sister won.

OTHER USES OF COMMAS

13n **Use a comma to separate items in dates and addresses.**

EXAMPLES   On Wednesday, **January 1, 2020,** I'm having a party.
Reply to 92 Keystone Crossings, **Indianapolis,** IN 46240.

NOTE   Commas are not placed between the month and the day, between the house number and the street name, or between the two-letter state code and the ZIP Code.

13o **Use a comma after the salutation of a friendly letter and after the closing of any letter.**

EXAMPLES   Dear Luis,   Yours truly,

13p **Use a comma before an abbreviation such as *Jr., St.,* or *M.D.* following a name and also after the abbreviation when the name and the abbreviation are used together in a sentence.**

EXAMPLES   Felice Wilson**, J.D.**
Isn't that Wilson Root, **Jr.,** in that car?

13q **Do not use unnecessary commas.**

Use a comma only when a rule requires one or if the meaning is unclear without one.

INCORRECT   The girl in my homeroom who plays bass with the orchestra, is from Kiev.
[*Girl,* the subject, must not be separated from its verb *is.*]

CORRECT   The girl in my homeroom who plays bass with the orchestra is from Kiev.

EXERCISE 8   Proofreading Sentences for Correct Use of Commas

For each of the following sentences, insert commas where needed, and draw a line through any commas that are misplaced. If a sentence is correct, write C on the line before the sentence.

EX. _____ 1. The winner/of the award/was Alex Wong, CPA.

_____ 1. The movie credits listed the hero's name as "King Kong Sr."

_____ 2. End the message, "Yours truly Renata".

_____ 3. On Saturday April 25 2020, we're having a class reunion.

_____ 4. I sent congratulations to Shirley Draper Ph.D.

_____ 5. John Craig lived at 15 Cedar Street Colorado Springs Colorado.

_____ 6. The type of string that works best with this kite is sold here.

_____ 7. Mail twenty-five cents and the coupon to the cereal company in Battle Creek Michigan.

_____ 8. Bill Jr. looks just like Bill Sr.

_____ 9. The invitation began, "Dear Remi Can you come...."

_____ 10. During the 2000s one of the fastest growing U.S. metropolitan areas, was Las Vegas Nevada.

_____ 11. Someone whom you know arrived today.

_____ 12. A researcher sent the results to Los Angeles Harbor College Wilmington CA 90744.

_____ 13. The sign on the door, Frederick Hong M.D. was freshly painted.

_____ 14. She sent a letter to the Moon Institute of Technology 84 Crescent View, Solar System 203, Milky Way.

_____ 15. We attended the graduation of Susan Sakamoto J.D.

_____ 16. On July 4 2015, I saw the best fireworks display of my life.

_____ 17. The toothpaste that I like the most is in my suitcase.

_____ 18. Our school is located at Roger Williams Avenue Highland Park IL 60035.

_____ 19. The car that Geoff was driving, crossed the finish line first.

_____ 20. The show first aired at 9:30 P.M. on Thursday March 31.

_____ 21. The return address read 3495 Main St. Mobile AL 36601.

_____ 22. We're going to a wedding on the ninth of May.

_____ 23. An attorney needs a J.D., to practice in this state.

_____ 24. The notebook with the blue ribbon on it, is mine.

_____ 25. The card was signed, "Best wishes Helen, Sen, and Carlita Armstrong."

MODULE 13: PUNCTUATION

MODULE REVIEW

A. Proofreading Sentences for Correct Punctuation

For each of the sentences below, insert commas, periods, and other end marks where needed, and draw a line through any commas that are misplaced. If a sentence is correct, write *C* on the line before the sentence.

EX. _____ 1. Quick, bring me the 35-ft rope

_____ 1. Dr Pines lived at 59 Sagebrush Ave Tucson Ariz

_____ 2. Lonato played the drums Motega played the xylophone and Kibbe played the flute

_____ 3. The fourteen people, who hadn't known they would be, chosen stood up.

_____ 4. Were you born at 5:00 A M or 10:00 P M

_____ 5. She ended the letter, "Sincerely yours Karen Q O'Connell."

_____ 6. Katya planted lilacs daisies and daffodils but Bruno preferring trees planted ten 5-ft maples.

_____ 7. After hiking in the winter, they huddled by the fireplace.

_____ 8. Get out of that rain Shawn before you catch cold

_____ 9. The batter swung connected and hit the pitch over the center field wall

_____ 10. Did you watch the special on PBS the Public Broadcasting System?

_____ 11. She bet that no one would believe it and they didn't

_____ 12. Before you could blink your eye the lemonade was gone

_____ 13. Ms Jackson the grocer's wife sometimes gave out free apples on Sundays; so we were always sure to be there just in case

_____ 14. Limping along, Claude was glad the hike was over.

_____ 15. Yikes what a fish

_____ 16. Proud of their new boat Jeff and Walter named it, the J W Flash

_____ 17. Naturally you can ask Masako; but Akio who was there earlier may be able to tell you more about it

_____ 18. Happy enthusiastic energetic we set out on the long voyage

_____ 19. Lionel catch that falling plate of tamales before they are ruined

_____ 20. Tired from a long day in the woods the lumberjack in the heavy plaid jacket sat down to speak to his friend Jody

B. Correcting Punctuation in a Paragraph

In the paragraph below, add end marks and commas where needed. Draw a line through any punctuation marks that are misplaced.

EX. [1] Did you know that sculptures can be made from clay, stone, wood, or metal?

[1] Some artists make sculptures by building them out of various materials, and others create them, by carving them out of solid blocks of stone wood or other hard substances. [2] The earliest known sculptures were made in the Stone Age about thirty thousand years ago [3] By 3000 B C sculptors, in Middle Eastern civilizations, were making fine stone carvings *in relief* that is, with the figures standing out a bit from a flat background. [4] During the time of the ancient Greeks and Romans sculptors made statues of their gods and goddesses; but they also sculpted men women athletes soldiers and lawmakers. [5] Modern sculptors who tend to emphasize shape rather than reality in their work have used moving parts to add a whole new dimension to the art form.

C. Working Cooperatively to Write a Letter

You are living in the year 2820 on the planet Discor. You can speak and write in English, and you have a new pen pal on Earth. Work with a partner to write a letter describing a sports event you have recently attended on Discor. Create an explanation of the rules, setting, and equipment for one of the games listed below. Or you may devise a game of your own. Remember that what you describe will be totally unknown to your pen pal, so you'll have to use restrictive and nonrestrictive phrases and clauses in your explanation of the game. Be sure to use end marks and commas correctly.

Speed Rings	Combat Ball	Star Words	Crater Hop
Planet Diving	Star Chase	Moon Zoom	Warp Walk

EX. Crater Hop

Dear Ricardo,

Last week, I saw a Crater Hopping Contest, a game that is popular here on Discor. In this game, for young and old alike, players compete with each other by bouncing from one crater to another.

14a Use a semicolon alone between closely related independent clauses if they are not joined by *and, but, for, nor, or, so,* or *yet*.

EXAMPLE   Joyce's favorite group was coming to town; she was standing in line to buy concert tickets.

14b Use a semicolon between independent clauses joined by conjunctive adverbs or transitional expressions. Also use a semicolon (rather than a comma) between independent clauses joined by a coordinating conjunction when the clauses contain commas.

EXAMPLES   Joleen decided not to take the shop class; **instead**, she would take the auto mechanics class.

Frank arrived early at the office; **for this reason**, he received the first interview appointment.

Jefferson washed the dog and the cat; he rinsed out the tub and mopped the floor; then he took a nap.

14c Use a colon before a list of items, especially after such expressions as *as follows* and *the following*.

EXAMPLES   For her birthday, Kay received several things she had been wanting: a new dress, the latest album by her favorite group, a red hat, and a silver bracelet.

Hall monitors are responsible for the following: picking up all trash, reporting hazards, and directing fire drills.

NOTE   Do not use a colon before a list that directly follows a verb or a preposition.

EXAMPLE   My favorite cartoonists are Robb Armstrong, Stephan Pastis, Scott Adams, and Charles Schultz.

14d Use a colon before a long, formal statement or quotation.

EXAMPLE   Grady stood at the podium before the town council and began his speech: "I am a citizen of this country. I am a resident of this state. I have lived in this town for seventeen years."

14e Use a colon between independent clauses when the second clause explains or restates the idea of the first.

EXAMPLE   Jacques decided to walk: he wanted to learn his way around the new neighborhood.

EXERCISE 1   Proofreading Sentences for Correct Use of Semicolons and Colons

Use a caret (∧) to show where a semicolon or colon is needed in each sentence below. Some sentences are correct.

EX.   1. Krista's boss asked her to order the following office supplies:∧a box of felt-tip pens, two reams of copy paper, twenty-five folders, and staples.

1. Lydia's father is a master chef he oversees the kitchen at a five-star restaurant.

2. That magazine contains articles on the Olmec people of Mexico, the Red Sea, Kodiak Island in Alaska, and Taiwan.

3. The mystery writer's latest book is sold out in all the neighborhood bookstores however, I was able to order a copy from the publisher.

4. The mayor concluded the debate with this statement "My worthy opponent, you have indeed presented a persuasive argument."

5. Carlotta asked for a large glass of ice water she was extremely thirsty after her run.

6. Tina was surprised when she was selected to play the lead in the junior class play she had expected only a minor role.

7. The arrow is an important part of traditional Crow culture older Crow men teach the younger men how to make and shoot the arrows.

8. In his backpack, Jaimie had the following items his notebook, a few pens and pencils, a baseball mitt, two tennis balls, a half-eaten pretzel, an empty box of raisins, and one sock.

9. Monroe ran into the house and sped up the stairs he took a shower and dressed then he ran down the stairs and out of the house.

10. Steve went to his room right after dinner he needed some time to be alone.

HYPHENS

14f   **Use a hyphen with compound numbers from *twenty-one* to *ninety-nine* and with fractions used as modifiers.**

   EXAMPLES thirty-seven people one-half cup of milk

14g   **Use a hyphen with the prefixes *ex–*, *self–*, *all–*, and *great–*; with the suffixes –*elect* and –*free;* and with all prefixes before a proper noun or a proper adjective.**

   EXAMPLES ex-senator self-confident all-important senator-elect pro-Arab

14h   **Hyphenate a compound adjective when it precedes the noun it modifies.**

   EXAMPLES a well-defined rule a rule that is well defined

   Do not use a hyphen if one of the modifiers before a noun is an adverb ending in –*ly*.

   EXAMPLE a **clearly stated** argument

EXERCISE 2   Proofreading Sentences for Correct Use of Hyphens

Use a caret (∧) to show where a hyphen is needed in each sentence below. Some sentences are correct.

   EX. 1. a well-groomed dog
                ∧

1.   a tender hearted man
2.   one fourth cup of water
3.   a storm in the mid Atlantic
4.   the new president elect
5.   a finely tuned instrument
6.   a world renowned tenor
7.   a clearly expressed point
8.   a pro consumer settlement
9.   one half of the class
10.   thirty four states

DASHES, PARENTHESES, AND BRACKETS

14i   **Use a dash to show an abrupt break in thought.**

EXAMPLES   And then Arnold showed up—what luck!

              Cameron, I want to tell you—and I really mean this—you've been a great friend.

14j   **Use a dash to mean *namely, in other words, that is*, and similar expressions that come before an explanation.**

EXAMPLE   I left for the reason I told you—I had to meet Cynthia to return her keys to her.

14k   **Use parentheses to enclose informative or explanatory material of minor importance. Be sure that the material can be omitted without losing important information or changing the basic meaning of the sentence.**

EXAMPLES   On our way to Amarillo (the only city anywhere near us), we stopped every twenty minutes.

              My nephew Neil (my sister's son) is directing the school play.

NOTE   A parenthetical sentence that falls within another sentence should not begin with a capital unless it begins with a word that should always be capitalized. It also should not end with a period but may end with a question mark or exclamation point.

EXAMPLE   Rosemary Apple Blossom Lonewolf **(have you heard of her?)** is a talented Native American potter.

14l   **Use brackets to enclose informative or explanatory material within quoted material.**

EXAMPLE   The doctor was yelling, "Get him two units [of blood], stat [fast]!"

EXERCISE 3   Using Dashes, Parentheses, and Brackets Correctly

In each of the following sentences, use a caret (∧) to add dashes, parentheses, and brackets where needed.

    EX.   1. Our new neightbors—actually, they moved in six months ago—are from Santiago, Chile.   ∧   ∧

1. My math teacher Mrs. Penta did you have her for math, too? expects all of us to be as excited and enthusiastic about equations as she is.

2. Two years after the first commercial radio station KDKA in Pittsburgh, Pennsylvania went on the air in 1920, five hundred stations were broadcasting across America.

3. Flo will do as you asked she will pick you up at the train station at exactly six o'clock.

4. Peter yelled up the stairs to Nina, "Toss me my mitt on the shelf in the closet, please."

5. Many of his friends actually, only two of them agree with his opinion about longer school days.

6. My sister Ellie whose real name is Elvira Maria was named for my great-grandmother who immigrated to America from Italy in the early 1900s.

7. The winner of the acoustic guitar competition there were more than 150 contestants was Paul Hunter.

8. Zimbabwe formerly known as Rhodesia, Southern Rhodesia, and Zimbabwe-Rhodesia is in the eastern half of southern Africa.

9. Instead of waffles my favorite breakfast food I ordered whole-grain muffins.

10. Some prepositions look at the list in Module 10 are compound.

11. People with *joie de vivre* literally, "joy of living" get enormous pleasure out of their lives.

12. Samuel Clemens 1835–1910, wrote under the pen name of Mark Twain worked as a riverboat pilot, a newspaper reporter, and a printer.

13. The door swung open and Marianna walked in what a shock!

14. There was a rumor going around school rumors spread like wildfire in a small town like this that Spike Lee was going to film a movie in our town.

15. The dog's barking although harmless seems endless.

16. We overheard Franco say, "Today his wedding day is the happiest day of my life."

17. The pages of the diary packed in a trunk for seventy-five years had yellowed and become brittle.

18. In 1846, The Know-Nothing Party it got its name because its members responded "I know nothing" to questions about the party was a secret organization that tried to keep foreign-born people from holding political office in America.

19. French physicist Marie Curie who was married to Pierre Curie won a Nobel Prize for chemistry and one for physics.

20. Jenna, I want to explain and I really hope you will understand why I missed your party.

UNDERLINING (ITALICS)

Italics are printed characters that slant to the right. Use *underlining* to indicate italics in handwritten or typewritten work.

14m **Underline (italicize) titles of books, plays, periodicals (magazines and newspapers), films, television programs, works of art, long musical compositions, trains, ships, aircraft, and spacecraft.**

Type of Name	Examples
Books	*Anything Goes, Julie of the Wolves*
Plays	*Oedipus the King, Hamilton*
Periodicals	*Arizona Daily Star, Outdoor Photographer*
Films	*Moana, It's A Wonderful Life*
Television Programs	*Amazing Race, American Idol*
Works of Art	*The Night Watch, The Cry*
Long Musical Compositions	*C-Minor Piano Trio, Turandot*
Trains	*Renaissance, TGV Atlantique*
Ships	*America, Intrepid*
Aircraft	*Kitty Hawk, Air Force One*
Spacecraft	*Soyuz 11, Endeavour*

NOTE   Italicize the title of a poem only if the poem is long enough to be published as a separate book. Such long poems are usually divided into titled or numbered sections. The titles of these sections are enclosed in quotation marks.

14n **Italicize (underline) foreign words and letters, words, and figures referred to as such.**

EXAMPLES   The *q.v.* in an encyclopedia stands for the Latin words *quod vide*, meaning "which see"
There are four *i*'s in *Mississippi*.
Make that *6* more readable if you can.

EXERCISE 4   Correcting Sentences with Underlining (Italics)

For each sentence below, underline the word or item that should be italicized.

EX.   1. This mystery story takes place on a train called the <u>Orient Express</u>.

1. The painting by Aaron Douglas on page 422 and the poem by James Weldon Johnson on the next page have the same title, which is The Creation.

2. His last name has every vowel in it except an a.

3. Do you know which actor played Dracula in the original film Dracula?

4. The French philosopher René Descartes wrote the Latin phrase cogito, ergo sum which means "I think, therefore I am."

5. Richard didn't think he would enjoy opera until he saw a production of Carmen.

6. The television program Kung Fu: The Legend Continues is a sequel to the old television show that also starred David Carradine.

7. In 1991, the crew of the submersible vessel Deep See discovered five United States Navy planes from the 1940s.

8. The audience helps decide the ending in the play Shear Madness.

9. All the major articles in an issue of National Geographic are listed on the cover.

10. I was disappointed by the ending of John Grisham's book, The Whistler.

11. Charles Lindbergh titled his Pulitzer Prize-winning book after his plane, the Spirit of St. Louis.

12. Did you see that incredible photograph on the front page of today's Arkansas Democrat-Gazette?

13. I saw the original painting Woman Doing Beadwork on Buckskin Shirt by the artist Blue Eagle when I visited my grandmother in Santa Fe, New Mexico, last year.

14. Did you notice that every phone number mentioned in that movie began with the numbers 555?

15. The music played during dinner was Beethoven's Piano Concerto No. 5.

MODULE 14: PUNCTUATION

QUOTATION MARKS

14o **Use quotation marks to enclose a *direct quotation*—a person's exact words. A direct quotation always begins with a capital letter.**

EXAMPLES   Jon's dad told us, **"S**tay off the phone!**"**

The Declaration of Independence begins, **"W**hen in the course of human events …**"**

Do not use quotations marks for an *indirect quotation*.

DIRECT QUOTATION   Billie asked, "May I help?" [Billie's exact words]
INDIRECT QUOTATION   Billie asked if she could help. [not Billie's exact words]

14p **When an expression such as *he said* divides a quoted sentence into two parts, the second part begins with a small letter.**

EXAMPLE   "I believe," Jorge said, **"t**hat that's a dual exhaust."

If the second part of a divided quotation is a new sentence, a period (not a comma) follows the interrupting expression. The second part then begins with a capital letter.

EXAMPLE   "Zack won't be here today," Arnold said. **"H**e has to take his sister to the doctor."

NOTE   An interrupting expression is not part of a quotation, so it should never be located inside the quotation marks.

INCORRECT   "Davis, Coach said, get in there and play defense."
CORRECT   "Davis**,**" Coach said, **"g**et in there and play defense."

14q **Separate a direct quotation from the rest of a sentence with a comma, a question mark, or an exclamation point, but not with a period.**

EXAMPLES   "Skye, if you're near it**,**" Sam said, "please hand me the hammer."

"Can you come over now**?**" Pearly asked.

"Super**!**" Stephen exclaimed.

14r **Always place commas and periods inside the closing quotation marks.**

EXAMPLE   "You know**,**" Shing said, "I'd like a chance, too**.**"

14s **Always place colons and semicolons outside the closing quotation marks.**

EXAMPLES   Sonja listed the extra ingredients in her "Veggie Surprise"**:** peas, tomatoes, squash, and mozzarella cheese.

Parthenia said, "I'm not doing anything for my birthday"**;** our plans for her surprise party were working.

14t Place question marks and exclamation points inside the closing quotation marks only if the quotation is a question or an exclamation. Otherwise, place them outside the closing quotation marks.

EXAMPLES "How do I get to Route 23?" Why did she say, "Synthetic"?
She yelled, "Ouch!" I hate it when he says, "Okay"!

NOTE In a question or an exclamation that ends with a quotation, only the question mark or exclamation point is necessary, and it is placed outside the closing quotation marks.

14u When writing *dialogue* (a conversation), begin a new paragraph each time the speaker changes, and enclose each speaker's words in quotation marks.

EXAMPLE "Dad, can I go with Lok after school?" Winnie asked.
"May I," he answered.
"Dad, may I go with Lok after school?"
"Well," he said, "where were you planning on going?"
"To the marsh," she replied. "Phoebe heard there was a gigantic stork there, and we want to see it."

14v Use single quotation marks to enclose a quotation within a quotation.

EXAMPLE Joel said, "I thought I heard you say, 'There's one more roll left.'" [Notice that the period is placed inside the single quotation mark.]

14w Use quotation marks to enclose titles of short works, such as short stories, poems, essays, articles, songs, episodes of television series, and modules and other parts of books.

Type of Name	Examples	
Short Stories	"The Circuit"	"Everybody Knows Tobie"
Poems	"Braly Street"	"The Lesson of Walls"
Essays	"River Notes"	"Rattlesnake Hunt"
Articles	"Strong Medicine"	"Breaking a Sound Barrier"
Songs	"Under African Skies"	"Stardust"
TV Episodes	"Barbara the Mom"	"Shadows in a Desert Sea"
Modules and Parts of Books	"Drama"	"Historical Introduction"

EXERCISE 5   Correcting Sentences by Adding Quotation Marks and Other Puctuation Marks

In each of the sentences below, add quotation marks and other marks of punctuation where needed. Capital letters may also be needed.

EX.   1. **"I have trouble memorizing poetry,"** Chloe said.

1. Tom said That's probably because you try to learn it line by line instead of sentence by sentence

2. Can you explain that more clearly asked Chloe.

3. Cathy raised her hand and answered I can

4. Do you remember Naoshi's poem that begins She looks to the towering mountains Miss Stuart asked

5. Tom said That's the one in which the list of chores is compared to a mountain range he was obviously familiar with the poem

6. Although there are three stanzas in that poem Cathy said there are only three sentences in the entire poem.

7. So what Chloe questioned

8. Look at each sentence Tom said Think about what each sentence is saying Thinking about each sentence will help you understand the poem. Understanding it should help you memorize it To quote Miss Stuart You have to read poetry on two levels, the figurative and the literal

9. Figurative language uses imagery and other figures of speech to convey meanings Miss Stuart explained

10. What terrific imagery Fred used in his poem that begins with the sentence Dinosaurs are not always prehistoric Cathy exclaimed

11. What two things are compared in that poem asked Tom

12. A comparison is made between a dinosaur and a Model T answered Cathy

13. How wild Chloe said I can't believe that I thought poetry was boring Miss Stuart told me that if I learned how to read poetry, I would enjoy it more

14. Chloe, if you get a chance Tom said read The Fish by Elizabeth Bishop Also you might find it helpful to read the module Personal Response to Literature

15. Chloe answered You're right. I thought I heard Miss Stuart say There will be a free-reading period tomorrow

EXERCISE 6   Proofreading Sentences

Proofread the sentences below for correct use of quotation marks, other marks of punctuation, and capitalization. Draw a line through each error, and add any missing punctuation marks or capitalization where needed. Some sentences may be correct.

EX.   1.   **"I'll give you a clue,"** Mrs. Spinazola said. "you name the holiday and give me one fact about that holiday**."**

1.   "Will we be graded on this" Art asked.

2.   Mrs. Spinazola just smiled and said "a song you might hear on this holiday contains the words "He stuck a feather in his cap"

3.   Trina said "Would that happen to be Independence Day she was trying to be funny

4.   "Trina, can you give us one interesting fact about that day?" asked Mrs. Spinazola.

5.   "You bet she exclaimed!"

6.   "I believe, she said "that Independence Day celebrates the day on which the Continental Congress approved the Declaration of Independence."

7.   Lynette added John Adams said "It ought to be solemnized with pomp and parade, with shows, games, sports."

8.   "Great" Mrs. Spinazola said. Now I'll give you a clue about another holiday."

9.   She said "this holiday is celebrated the last week of December by many African American families

10.   "Is it Kwanzaa." asked Lloyd?

11.   Lloyd said that Kwanzaa is a relatively new holiday, a time for a family to share memories; it was first celebrated in 1966.

12.   "Kwanzaa is a seven-day celebration Lloyd added "It is a time for African Americans to focus on their heritage."

13.   "Sandra, if you can Mrs. Spinazola said please explain some of the symbols of Kwanzaa."

14.   Many of the symbols, like the bowl of fruit, vegetables, and nuts, are similar to those used at harvest festivals Sandra said.

15.   As my friend Marissa told me the kikombe, or unity cup, is a special cup that the whole family drinks from each night Sandra added.

MODULE 14: PUNCTUATION
MODULE REVIEW

A.   Correcting Sentences by Adding Punctuation Marks

In the sentences below, add correct punctuation where it is needed.

EX.   1. Lenore sings only when she works outside by herself she doesn't think anyone else should have to listen.

1. Todd looked around at the nurses and doctors who had come to say goodbye and said I want to thank you for everything you've done. Without your help and your care, I might not be walking out of here today on my own two feet. Thank you so much.

2. Mr. Julius looked toward the back of the room students who arrived late always stood there and said Please stop that commotion right now.

3. I think Annie said that the writings of Dave Barry, a former newspaper columnist from Florida are some of the funniest that I have ever read.

4. A series of devastating fires struck the community just as it was recovering from an earlier disaster terrible floods.

5. Students were asked to bring the following items to the school lock-up a sleeping bag, a pillow, a midnight snack, a toothbrush, a change of clothes, and a book or a game.

6. Who would like to volunteer at the senior center after school the principal asked

7. The Emancipation Proclamation begins, Whereas, on the twenty-second day of September, in the year of our Lord one thousand eight hundred and sixty-two …

8. A recent television showing of the movie Dances with Wolves included film footage that had not been released before.

9. My older sister is a musician Chan said She just got a job teaching band in a grade school.

10. Yikes Ethan yelled You almost ran over my toe with that thing.

11. Paul asked What did Franco mean when he said Revolutionary

12. How did you like reading Shakespeare's play Much Ado About Nothing Tina asked.

13. Mr. Jensen said, Five years ago today February 6, 2015 we had ten inches of snow.

14. Joanie said My baby brother made us laugh last night when he said Knock, knock, who's there? and then he started to laugh as if he had finished the joke.

15. In his closing remarks, the coach said, Thank you again for this the engraved trophy, and thank you for all the support you have given me.

B. Proofreading a Dialogue for Errors in Punctuation and Capitalization

Correct the punctuation and capitalization errors in the dialogue below. On your own paper, rewrite the dialogue correctly. Remember to begin a new paragraph each time the speaker changes.

EX.   [1] Tomás and I were racing to the train station to catch the
      R   E
      ~~r~~ed-eye ~~e~~xpress; it was the last train home.

[1] When we had taken our seats on the train we were lucky to find two together Tomás said, "so what did you think of the movie." [2] We had just streamed the movie The Fugitive, starring Harrison Ford. [3] Terrific I said However, I'm experiencing various emotions confusion, excitement, surprise. [4] Did you see that article that was published recently it must have been on the internet about the filming of that first scene. [5] Tomás said. "Wow! that train wreck at the beginning was unbelievable. [6] I turned to Tomas. [7] "You know, I said they destroyed a real train for that scene in the beginning of the movie. [8] "Can you imagine, I continued, how much that must have cost." [9] Filming the scene must have cost a fortune! [10] Then I added I think I remember reading that they could only shoot that scene once as a result, it had to be good."

C. Writing a Vacation Journal

During your vacation to Hawaii, you attended a luau. On your own paper, record your impressions and observations including some of the comments you overheard. You might include statements about clothing, flowers, decorations, food, and entertainment. Before you begin writing, look in encyclopedias and research your topic. Then write at least fifteen sentences using, at least once, each of the punctuation marks discussed in the module: semicolons, colons, dashes, parentheses, brackets, italics, quotation marks, and commas and end marks used with quotations.

EX.   *July 7, 2020—We dressed in flowered shirts; and skirts; we ate tropical fruits and vegetables and sipped sweet juices; then we danced to the music.*

A dictionary entry is divided into several parts. Study the parts of the following sample dictionary entry.

> 1 2 3 4 5
> **neat** (nēt), *adj.*, **–er**, **–est** [French *net,* clean < Latin *nitidus,* bright, fine]
> 6 7
> **1.** in a well-ordered condition [a *neat* room] **2.** having a simple, attractive
> appearance [a *neat* dresser] **3.** clever or appropriate [a *neat* story]
> 8 9
> **4.** INFORMAL superlative in every way [What a *neat* collection!] **–neat'•ly,**
> 9 10
> *adv.* **–neat'ness,** *n. SYN. **Neat*** suggests "order and an absence of unnecessary
> details." ***Tidy*** means "orderly." ***Trim*** suggests "neat and stylish." *ANT.*
> disorderly, messy

1. **Entry word.** The entry word shows the correct spelling of a word. An alternate spelling may also be shown. The entry word shows how the word should be divided into syllables and may also show whether the word should be capitalized.

2. **Pronunciation.** The pronunciation is shown using accent marks, phonetic symbols, or diacritical marks. Each *phonetic symbol* represents a specific sound. *Diacritical marks* are special symbols placed above letters to show how those letters sound.

3. **Part-of-speech labels.** These labels are usually abbreviated and show how the entry word should be used in a sentence. Some words may be used as more than one part of speech. In such a case, a part-of-speech label is also given before the set of definitions that matches each label.

4. **Other forms.** Sometimes a dictionary shows spellings of plural forms of nouns, tenses of verbs, or the comparative forms of adjectives and adverbs.

5. **Etymology.** The *etymology* tells how a word (or its parts) entered the English language. The etymology also shows how the word has changed over time.

6. **Definitions.** If there is more than one meaning, definitions are numbered or lettered.

7. **Sample usage.** Some dictionaries include sample phrases to illustrate particular meanings of words.

8. **Special usage labels.** These labels identify how a word is used (*Slang*), how common a word is (*Rare*), or how a word is used in a special field, such as botany (*Bot.*).

9. **Related word forms.** These are forms of the entry word created by adding suffixes or prefixes. Sometimes dictionaries also list common phrases in which the word appears.

10. **Synonyms and antonyms.** Words similar in meaning are ***synonyms***. Words opposite in meaning are ***antonyms***. Many dictionaries list synonyms and antonyms at the ends of some word entries.

EXERCISE 1 Using a Dictionary

Use a dictionary to answer the questions below.

EX. 1. How many syllables are in the word *multiplication*? <u>*five*</u>

1. How is the word *flirtatious* divided into syllables? _____

2. What is the spelling for the plural form of *echo*? _____

3. Give three different meanings for the word *light*. _____

    _____

4. What is the past tense of *outwit*? _____

5. What is the etymology of the word *Mayday*? _____

    _____

EXERCISE 2 Writing Words with Alternate Spellings

For each of the words below, write the alternate spelling on the line after the word.

EX. 1. dialogue <u>*dialog*</u>

1. rigor   _____   4. calif   _____

2. phoney _____   5. gemology _____

3. litre   _____

SPELLING RULES

ie and *ei*

15a Write *ie* when the sound is long *e*, except after *c*.

  EXAMPLES ach**ie**ve, br**ie**f, c**ei**ling, pr**ie**st, rec**ei**pt, y**ie**ld
  EXCEPTIONS l**ei**sure, n**ei**ther, s**ei**ze, w**ei**rd

15b Write *ei* when the sound is not long *e*, especially when the sound is long *a*.

  EXAMPLES b**ei**ge, h**ei**ght, n**ei**ghbor, r**ei**ndeer, sl**ei**gh
  EXCEPTIONS anc**ie**nt, fr**ie**nd, p**ie**, qu**ie**t, sc**ie**nce

–cede, –ceed, and *–sede*

15c The only word ending in *–sede* is *supersede*. The only words ending in *–ceed* are *exceed, proceed,* and *succeed.* All other words with this sound end in *–cede.*

  EXAMPLES ac**cede**, inter**cede**, pre**cede**, re**cede**, se**cede**

EXERCISE 3 Writing Words with *ie* and *ei*

On the line in each word below, write the letters *ie* or *ei* to spell the word correctly. Use a dictionary as needed.

EX. 1. bel __*ie*__ ve

1. perc _____ ve
2. shr _____ k
3. bes _____ ge
4. pl _____ rs
5. v _____ n
6. br _____ f
7. fr _____ ght
8. h _____ ght
9. n _____ ce
10. counterf _____ t

11. t _____ r
12. cash _____ r
13. ch _____ f
14. dec _____ ve
15. forf _____ t
16. th _____ f
17. f _____ ld
18. v _____ l
19. p _____ ce
20. rec _____ ve

21. r _____ gn
22. rel _____ f
23. th _____ r
24. w _____ ld
25. p _____ rce
26. front _____ r
27. for _____ gn
28. y _____ ld
29. w _____ gh
30. _____ ght

EXERCISE 4   Proofreading a Paragraph to Correct Spelling Errors

The following paragraph contains ten spelling errors. Underline the misspelled words, and write the correct spelling above each misspelled word.

                                  received

EX.   [1] Bicycle racing first <u>recieved</u> wide notice after the development of the safety bike.

[1] In the United States, enthusiasm for bicycle racing reached a new hieght at the turn of the century. [2] For a breif time, bicycle racing was even more popular than baseball. [3] In 1896, it acheived even higher status by being included in the Olympics. [4] Some of the speed records posted by the first cyclists are unbeleivable. [5] For example, we would have to conceed that for a racer to cover a mile in sixty seconds is amazing. [6] Charles "Mile-a-Minute" Murphy succeded in doing just that in 1889, by riding his bike behind a train. [7] The train was fitted with a large windsheild so that Murphy encountered very little air resistance. [8] Still, no one can say Murphy was moving at a liesurely pace. [9] In 1926, the Belgian cyclist Leon Vanderstuyft siezed a world record by racing over seventy-six miles in one hour. [10] Modern racers would have difficulty superseeding such a feat even in ideal conditions.

A *prefix* is a letter or a group of letters added to the beginning of a word to change its meaning.

15d   When adding a prefix to a word, do not change the spelling of the word itself.

EXAMPLES   re + write = **re**write   un + natural = **un**natural
            in + correct = **in**correct   under + rate = **under**rate

A *suffix* is a letter or a group of letters added to the end of a word to change its meaning.

15e   When adding the suffix *–ness* or *–ly* to a word, do not change the spelling of the word itself.

EXAMPLES   kind + ness = kind**ness**   quick + ness = quick**ness**
            bold + ly = bold**ly**   clear + ly = clear**ly**

EXCEPTION   For most words that end in *y*, change the *y* to *i* before adding *–ly* or *–ness*.

            EXAMPLES   silly + ness = sill**iness**   merry + ly = merr**ily**

15f   Drop the final silent *e* before a suffix beginning with a vowel.

Vowels are the letters *a, e, i, o, u,* and sometimes *y*. All other letters of the alphabet are *consonants*.

EXAMPLES   vote + er = vot**er**   drive + ing = driv**ing**
            note + able = not**able**   dose + age = dos**age**

EXCEPTIONS Keep the final silent *e*.
            • in a word ending in *ce* or *ge* before a suffix beginning with *a* or *o:*
                        trac**eable**   outrag**eous**
            • in *dye* before *–ing:*   dy**eing**
            • in *mile* before *–age:*   mil**eage**

15g   Keep the final silent *e* before a suffix beginning with a consonant.

EXAMPLES   love + ly = lov**ely**   time + less = time**less**
            pure + ly = pure**ly**   wise + ly = wise**ly**

EXCEPTIONS true + ly = tru**ly**   judge + ment = judg**ment**
            nine + th = nin**th**   argue + ment = argu**ment**
            acknowledge + ment = acknowledg**ement** *or* acknolwedg**ment**

EXERCISE 5   Spelling Words with Prefixes and Suffixes

On the lines below, complete the word problems by adding the given prefix or suffix to the word.

EX.   1.   dis + belief   _disbelief_

1.   up + hold   _____
2.   taste + ful   _____
3.   argue + ment   _____
4.   im + movable   _____
5.   busy + ly   _____
6.   re + tell   _____
7.   simple + er   _____
8.   mis + spell   _____
9.   manage + ment   _____
10. courage + ous   _____

11. mile + age   _____
12. fame + ous   _____
13. dis + appear   _____
14. haste + y   _____
15. ready + ly   _____
16. bake + ed   _____
17. sub + topic   _____
18. re + cycle   _____
19. nine + ty   _____
20. final + ly   _____

EXERCISE 6   Spelling Words with Suffixes

On the lines below, complete the word problems by adding the given suffix to the word.

EX.   1.   legal + ly   _legally_

1.   normal + ly   _____
2.   change + ed   _____
3.   quote + able   _____
4.   adventure + ous   _____
5.   loud + ness   _____
6.   believe + ing   _____
7.   heavy + ness   _____
8.   simple + est   _____
9.   notice + able   _____
10. calculate + or   _____

11. mere + ly   _____
12. race + er   _____
13. messy + ness   _____
14. sure + est   _____
15. love + ly   _____
16. care + less   _____
17. make + ing   _____
18. dense + ly   _____
19. lively + er   _____
20. scrape + ing   _____

15h   **For words ending in *y* preceded by a consonant, change the *y* to *i* before any suffix that does not begin with *i*.**

EXAMPLES   carry + ing = carry**ing**   vary + ous = var**ious**
                   funny + est = funn**iest**   magnify + ing = magnify**ing**

EXCEPTIONS   dry + ness = dry**ness**   sly + ly = sly**ly**

15i   **For words ending in *y* preceded by a vowel, keep the *y* when adding a suffix.**

EXAMPLES   play + ed = play**ed**   enjoy + ment = enjoy**ment**
                   joy + ful = joy**ful**   stay + ed = stay**ed**

EXCEPTIONS   day + ly = dai**ly**   pay + ed = pa**id**

15j   **Double the final consonant before a suffix that begins with a vowel if the word (1) has only one syllable or has the accent on the last syllable *and* (2) ends in a single consonant preceded by a single vowel.**

EXAMPLES   bat + er = ba**tt**er   concur + ent = concu**rr**ent
                   skip + ing = ski**pp**ing   red + est = re**dd**est

NOTE   The final consonant of some words may or may not be doubled. Either spelling is acceptable.

EXAMPLES   cancel + ed = cance**l**ed *or* cance**ll**ed
                   travel + er = trave**l**er *or* trave**ll**er

EXERCISE 7   Spelling Words with Suffixes

On your own paper, complete the word problems below by adding the given suffix to the word.

EX.   1. big + est
          1. *biggest*

1. pitch + er
2. ship + ing
3. rely + able
4. boy + hood
5. seem + ed

6. cry + ed
7. wrap + ed
8. sunny + est
9. win + ing
10. crazy + er

11. hurry + ing
12. mystery + ous
13. obey + ing
14. fly + ing
15. refer + ed

16. thin + er
17. begin + er
18. dark + est
19. glory + ous
20. marry + ed

EXERCISE 8   Proofreading to Correct Spelling in a Paragraph

In the paragraph below, underline the twenty spelling errors. Write the correct spelling above each misspelled word.

packing

EX.   [1] Houdini's best trick was his escape from the <u>packking</u> case.

[1] Harry Houdini, perhaps the most famous magician in history, bafflled everyone with this trick. [2] Handcufed inside a nailed and ropped-up crate, he then had a tugboat lower him by crane deep into the river. [3] The crowd waited and worryed as the minutes pased. [4] But suddenly, he reappearred, having done what everyone thought impossible. [5] The packing case had reemerged with Houdini siting triumphantly on top. [6] The case itself seemmed undamaged. [7] It looked as though Houdini had mysteryously conquerred the laws of nature. [8] But today, we know he had foolled the audience by inventting a clever illusion. [9] Houdini wore fake handcuffs, which he openned with a secret spring. [10] He also had slily tucked away a pair of nail cuters, with which he pried the case apart from inside. [11] Two of his men fixxed the case later. [12] When the tugboat was out of sight, they extractted the broken nails and replaced them with new ones. [13] Still, it was hard to witness the trick and not be impresed. [14] Houdini had to be both highly skiled and quite brave in order to accomplish it. [15] There is no deniing he was one of the greatest entertainers of all time.

PLURALS OF NOUNS

15k **Form the plurals of most nouns by adding –s.**

SINGULAR   dollar   height   idea   key   rope   mountain

PLURAL   dollars   heights   ideas   keys   ropes   mountains

15l **Form the plurals of nouns ending in s, x, z, ch, or sh by adding –es.**

SINGULAR   address   church   ranch   waltz   wish

PLURAL   addresses   churches   ranches   waltzes   wishes

NOTE   Proper nouns usually follow these rules, too.

EXAMPLES   the Martins   the Espositos
                  the Rosses   the Goodriches

EXERCISE 9   Spelling the Plurals of Nouns

On the line after each noun below, write the correct plural form.

EX.   1. hunch   _hunches_

1. dress   _____
2. skier   _____
3. sign   _____
4. trick   _____
5. Burns   _____
6. present   _____
7. task   _____
8. stress   _____
9. willow   _____
10. six   _____
11. lunch   _____
12. college   _____
13. fez   _____

14. arena   _____
15. stitch   _____
16. fox   _____
17. Toscanini   _____
18. flash   _____
19. wasp   _____
20. brush   _____
21. López   _____
22. fence   _____
23. climber   _____
24. shoe   _____
25. piano   _____

15m Form the plurals of nouns ending in *y* preceded by a consonant by changing the *y* to *i* and adding *–es.*

SINGULAR	century	fly	lady	penny	twenty
PLURAL	centur**ies**	fl**ies**	lad**ies**	penn**ies**	twent**ies**

EXCEPTION   With proper nouns, simply add *–s.*
  EXAMPLES   the Brady**s,** the Olinsky**s**

15n Form the plurals of nouns ending in *y* preceded by a vowel by adding *–s.*

SINGULAR	bay	display	key	Thursday	alley	toy
PLURAL	bay**s**	display**s**	key**s**	Thursday**s**	alley**s**	toy**s**

15o Form the plurals of most nouns ending in *f* by adding *–s.* The plurals of some nouns ending in *f* or *fe* are formed by changing the *f* to *v* and adding either *–s* or *–es.*

SINGULAR	belief	gulf	reef	life	shelf	wolf
PLURAL	belief**s**	gulf**s**	reef**s**	li**ves**	shel**ves**	wol**ves**

NOTE   When you are not sure how to spell the plural of a noun ending in *f* or *fe,* look in a dictionary.

EXERCISE 10   Spelling the Plurals of Nouns

On the line after each noun below, write the correct plural form.

EX.   1. leaf   *leaves*

1. blueberry   _____
2. Ripley   _____
3. thief   _____
4. way   _____
5. history   _____
6. roof   _____
7. country   _____
8. boy   _____
9. Monday   _____
10. half   _____

11. Kandinsky   _____
12. wharf   _____
13. folly   _____
14 display   _____
15. community   _____
16. story   _____
17. knife   _____
18. donkey   _____
19. kidney   _____
20. rally   _____

15p **Form the plurals of nouns ending in _o_ preceded by a vowel by adding _–s_. Form the plurals of nouns ending in _o_ preceded by a consonant by adding _–es_.**

SINGULAR	barrio	igloo	studio	echo	hero
PLURAL	barrio**s**	igloo**s**	studio**s**	echo**es**	hero**es**

EXCEPTIONS	hello**s**	tuxedo**s**

Form the plurals of most musical terms ending in _o_ by adding _–s_.

SINGULAR	alto	cello	solo	soprano
PLURAL	alto**s**	cello**s**	solo**s**	soprano**s**

NOTE   To form the plurals of some nouns ending in _o_ preceded by a consonant, you may add either _–s_ or _–es_.

SINGULAR	banjo	tornado	zero
PLURAL	banjo**s**	tornado**s**	zero**s**
	_or_	_or_	_or_
	banjo**es**	tornado**es**	zero**es**

NOTE   If you are ever in doubt about the plural form of a noun ending in _o_ preceded by a consonant, check the spelling in a dictionary.

15q **The plurals of a few nouns are formed in irregular ways.**

SINGULAR	tooth	woman	foot	child	goose
PLURAL	t**ee**th	w**o**men	f**ee**t	child**ren**	g**ee**se

15r **Form the plural of a compound noun consisting of a noun plus a modifier by making the modified noun plural.**

SINGULAR	disc jockey	football	brother-in-law	runner-up
PLURAL	disc jockey**s**	football**s**	brother**s**-in-law	runner**s**-up

EXERCISE 11   Spelling the Plurals of Nouns

On the line after each noun below, write the correct plural form.

EX.   1. photo _photos_

1. piccolo _____
2. goose _____
3. tomato _____
4. mouse _____
5. flamingo _____

6. man-of-war _____
7. Silvano _____
8. tooth _____
9. radio _____
10. mother-in-law _____

EXERCISE 12   Proofreading to Correct Spelling in Sentences

In the sentences below, underline all misspelled words. Write the correct spelling above each misspelled word.

children

EX.   1. All of the <u>childs</u> in the international chorus visited our school.

1. Smart drivers fasten their seats belt.

2. In the 1940s, our grandparents, listening to their radioes, heard singers performing

    soloes.

3. The President sometimes vetos the bills approved by Congress.

4. During the battle, our torpedos sunk three enemy man-of-wars.

5. Have you ever heard bongoses being played?

6. The mans lined themselves up quickly.

7. Celloes are much larger than piccolos.

8. My sister-in-laws gave me a surprise party.

9. Roberta fed bread crumbs to the gooses on the riverbank.

10. Most recording studioes have pianos.

EXERCISE 13   Using Plurals Correctly

On your own paper, write twenty sentences, using the plural forms of the words below.

EX.   1. ox
      1. *We saw oxen pulling carts at the state fair.*

1. motto	7. contralto
2. child	8. taco
3. Navajo	9. president-elect
4. seashell	10. sergeant-at-arms
5. eleventh-grader	11. zero
6. foot	12. mambo

13. tooth

14. baby sitter

15. mother-in-law

16. silo

17. mouse

18. rodeo

19. woman

20. patio

A. Correcting Spelling Errors in Sentences

Underline all misspelled words in each sentence below. Then write the correct spelling above each misspelled word.

                                        winning

EX.   1. We were all happy that our team had a <u>wining</u> season.

1. Alex openned the drawer and took out two boxs of lightbulbs.

2. The Frederickes took us to see the tennis matchs.

3. Why spend so much money for a car that can excede the speed limit?

4. The raceing boats crosed the finish line.

5. On our block, the Espositoes are fameous for their wonderful partys.

6. During our trip to Hollywood, we toured two film studioes.

7. Betty laughed and said, "I've got the coollest new jacket!"

8. Donald is a duck, but Mickey and Minnie are both mouses.

9. In those dayes, ships entering the harbor had to watch for reeves.

10. Undereporting income on your tax forms is a felony.

11. The nieghborhood committee told us to turn off our radioes after ten o'clock.

12. Who said the fashions of the seventies were timless?

13. We barly had time to put on our costumes.

14. After sending Roger out to buy three loafs of bread, I waitted for hours.

15. The navigateor usually sits next to the pilot in an airplane.

16. The stars of ice shows have to be gracful dancers as well as excellent skatters.

17. My mother finds amusment parks frivolous.

18. Those boyes ran off with all our blackberrys.

19. Most jurys don't work on Sundays.

20. Triing to guess the right answer all the time won't help you receive the best grade.

B. Proofreading a Paragraph to Correct Spelling Errors

Underline the misspelled words in the paragraph below, and write the correct spelling above each misspelled word. Some sentences contain more than one error. Some sentences are correct.

believe

EX.　[1] Can you <u>beleive</u> that seashells were once used as currency?

[1] For varyous reasons, money has taken many different forms throughout history.

[2] In Asia, bricks of tea were stampped with the name of a bank. [3] The Swedish

plate money peice is the largest metal coin in the world. [4] It wieghs forty-four

pounds, measureing twenty-four inches long. [5] Ornamental strings of shells were

eventually acceptted as money by European colonists and American Indians alike. [6]

Perhaps the most unusual type of currency was the stone money used by the people on

the island of Yap. [7] These Pacific islandders fashionned huge limestone disks to

serve as legal tender. [8] Thier size ranged from nine inches in diameter to as large as

twelve foots across. [9] Each coin had a hole in the middle so that it could be carried

on a pole. [10] Obviously, any thiefs on Yap had to plan very carefuly.

C. Writing a Language Workshop Lesson

You have won the district spelling championship and have been selected to teach your own English class a spelling lesson. Pick two of the spelling rules from this module to present to your class. On your own paper, write each rule and provide your own examples. Then, for each rule, make up an exercise so that your classmates will have a chance to practice the rule. Each exercise should contain at least five questions or items to complete. For each exercise, create a list of answers on a separate sheet of paper.

EX.   1. *RULE: Words ending in y preceded by a vowel do not change their spelling before a suffix.*

EXAMPLES: enjoy + ed = enjoyed   pay + ment = payment
gray + est = grayest   relay + ed = relayed

EXERCISE 1 Spelling Words with Suffixes
On your own paper, complete the word problem by adding the given suffix to the word.

EX.   1. *delay + ed*   1. *delayed*